KNOSSOS

A COMPLETE GUIDE TO THE PALACE OF MINOS

KNOSSOS

A COMPLETE GUIDE TO THE PALACE OF MINOS

ANNA MICHAILIDOU
Archaeologist

EKDOTIKE ATHENON S.A.
Athens 2001

ISBN 960-213-142-X

by

EKDOTIKE ATHENON S.A.

1, Vissarionos Street

Athens 106 72, Greece

PRINTED AND BOUND IN GREECE

by

EKDOTIKE HELLADOS S.A.

An affiliated company

8, Philadelphias Street, Athens

Publishers: George A. Christopoulos, John C. Bastias
Translation: Alexandra Doumas, Timothy Cullen
Managing Editor: Anna Michailidou
Layout: A. Simou, P. Pavlidou
Covers: A. Simou
Map and Plans prepared by T. Kotsoni
Special Photography: S. Tselentis, M. Skiadaresis,
S. Tsavdaroglou, N. Kontos

CONTENTS

INTRODUCTION

Knossos is located just 5 km. south-east of Herakleion — about ten minutes by car — on the hill of Kephala beside the Kairatos river (present-day Katsambas), amidst olive trees, vines and cypresses. It is the best known, most typical and most accessible part of Crete. Even if one has only a day to spare one can visit the palace of Knossos and the Herakleion Museum and so leave Crete with a general idea of its ancient civilisation.

Knossos was the most important town in Crete in prehistoric times. Homer speaks of the existence of one hundred cities in Crete at the time of the Trojan War and mentions Knossos first, then Gortyn, Miletos, Phaistos and others. He describes Knossos as "vast" and "a great city" and informs us that Minos was its king. The major excavations conducted in Crete since the end of the 19th century have brought to light the remains of a great civilisation, the first advanced civilisation in Europe. It spanned the interval between approximately 2800 and 1100 B.C. and Arthur Evans, the English excavator of Knossos, named it the Minoan Civilisation after the legendary Minos. The centre of the Minoan civilisation was Knossos, where excavations have revealed the actual palace of King Minos with its well-stocked magazines, royal apartments, shrines, the large central court and the throne room, in which the throne of Minos was discovered, the oldest throne in Europe.

The purpose of this guide is to help the visitor to find his way through the extremely complicated palace of Knossos, to give him an overall picture of the palace as it was in its heyday and to explain the specific function of each room, wherever this is possible. However, in order to understand the palace one should place it in its correct historical context,

◀ 1. *Minoan pithoi (storage jars) in the South Propylaeum.*

◀ 2. *Part of the palace of Knossos showing the South Propylaeum. In the background is the sacred Mt. Juktas.*

and so this guide aims at giving the reader a more general picture of the Minoan world.

The guide is divided into two sections. The first starts with a résumé of the mythological and historical background of Knossos, recounting the myths preserved by ancient tradition and in the writings of historians such as Herodotus and Thucydides. This is followed by a history of the excavations, which confirmed that behind the myths there was a basis of historical fact: the palace of Minos was found and within its corridors and courts the mythical figures of Ariadne and Theseus, Daidalos and the Minotaur came to life. The first section ends with the history of the palace, in the context of a general history of Crete: this explains who the Minoans were and where they lived, it enumerates the architectural phases through which the palace passed and it mentions the disasters and population movements both at Knossos and throughout the island.

The second section contains the actual guide to the site. It starts with a description of the topography of Knossos and the way to get there. Then comes a general plan of the palace and an account of the materials and principles employed in its construction, leading up to the tour of the palace itself. The aim of the tour is to explain the function of the different rooms, which is why some of the finds no longer visible *in situ* (they are in the Herakleion Museum) are frequently mentioned, since they help us to envisage the use of the place in which they were found. At appropriate points on the tour information is given about the Minoan way of life, script, religion, etc. The buildings around the palace of Knossos are examined afterwards.

Wherever there is a problem of dating, interpretation, cause of destruction, etc., the most generally accepted opinion is given. Frequently, however, reference is also made to contrary points of view so that the visitor will realise that there are no cut-and-dried answers. In archaeology, as in every science, there are always problems.

HISTORICAL OUTLINE

MYTH AND TRADITION

Crete is the setting for many of the Greek myths, most of them enacted in the elaborate and sumptuous palace of Knossos, where one figure stands out as dominant, the figure of King Minos.

> *Among their cities is the great city Cnosus, where Minos reigned*
> *when nine years old, he that held converse with great Zeus.*
> (*Od.* XIX. 178-9, Transl. A.T. Murray, Loeb Classical Library)

So sang Homer in the *Odyssey*. And the Athenian historian Thucydides speaks of Minos as the first known person to acquire a strong navy and control the greater part of the Greek sea; he expelled the Karians from the Cyclades, installed his sons as governors there and restricted piracy in the Aegean.

Minos was of divine origin, sired by the king of the gods himself, Zeus. In Phoenicia Zeus met Europa, daughter of the Phoenician king Agenor (or Phoinix), picking flowers with her friends by the sea-shore. He fell in love with her and in order to approach her transformed himself into a handsome, playful bull. The princess suspected nothing and mounted his back. The bull immediately plunged into the sea and brought her to Crete, and three sons — Minos, Rhadamanthys and Sarpedon — were duly born to Europa at Gortyn from her union with Zeus. Europa subsequently married Asterios, king of Crete, and after his death her son Minos reigned in Crete in accordance with laws given to him every nine years by his father, Zeus.

Minos married Pasiphae, daughter of Helios and the nymph Crete, who bore him four sons and four daughters. They lived in the palace of Knos-

3. Europa being abducted by Zeus in the guise of a bull, from a red-figure krater by the "Berlin painter". Early 5th cent. B.C. Tarquinia, Archaeological Museum.

sos, where many dramatic events took place. On one occasion Minos wished to offer a sacrifice to Poseidon and prayed to the god to send him a suitable victim. Poseidon sent him a fine white bull from the sea, but Minos chose to keep it and sacrificed another in its stead. Thus he incurred the wrath of the god, who, to punish him, aroused in the queen a consuming passion for the bull. In those days there lived at the court of Minos a very clever engineer, Daidalos. Daidalos fashioned a model of a cow in which he concealed the queen, who thus satisfied her love for the bull. Of their union was born a monster, the Minotaur, with a human body and bull's head, which lived in the Labyrinth, a complex structure which Daidalos built for it.

The myth continues with the journey of Androgeos, son of Minos, to Athens, where he participated in the games and won all the prizes, so incurring such envy that he was murdered. Minos mounted a campaign against Athens, conquered the neighbouring city of Megara, an Athenian ally, and in reprisal forced King Aegeus of Athens to send seven boys and seven girls annually (or every nine years) as food for the Minotaur in the Labyrinth.

A second important person now appears in the myth: Theseus, son of the Athenian King Aegeus (or of Poseidon). Theseus volunteered to join the third "death squad" along with thirteen other young Athenians, with the intention of slaying the Minotaur and freeing his people from this oppressive tribute to the Cretans. On arriving at Knossos he won the love of Ariadne, Minos' daughter, who asked Daidalos to help her to save her beloved. Daidalos showed her the way in and out of the Labyrinth and Ariadne gave Theseus the famous clew of thread, one end of which she tied to the entrance. Thus Theseus, after slaying the Minotaur, was able to find his way out of the Labyrinth. He took Ariadne and the other Athenian hostages and set sail for home. En route they visited Naxos, where they abandoned Ariadne asleep on the beach and went on to Athens without her. However, Dionysos, god of wine, fell in love with Ariadne and married her. They had three sons, Staphylos, Thoas and Oinopion.

Back at Knossos Minos vented his rage on Daidalos who, to escape it, fashioned wings for himself and his son Ikaros. With these they flew away, but Ikaros disregarded his father's advice not to fly too high and the sun melted the wax which held his feathers together. The youth fell from the sky and was drowned in the sea which bears his name (the Ikarian Sea). We next come across Daidalos at the city of Kamikos in Sicily, living at the court of its king Kokalos. Minos pursued him there, but Kokalos' daughters drowned him in a bath of scalding water. It is said that the king of Knossos was buried at the town of Minoa in Sicily, in a magnificent tomb with a temple on top of it. As he had been a great legislator in his lifetime, so in Hades he became one of the three judges of the underworld, along with Rhadamanthys and Aiakos.

4. These two mythical figures depicted on an oenochoe from Arkades have been tentatively identified as Theseus and Ariadne. 7th cent. B.C. Herakleion Museum.

5. *Theseus fighting the Minotaur, as illustrated on an Attic black-figure vase. The Athenian hero is shown grasping the monster's horns and plunging his sword into its body. 6th cent.* B.C. *Vatican Museum.*

6, 7. *On the return voyage from Crete Theseus' ship put in at Delos, where all the young men and girls went ashore and danced the sacred crane-dance. Detail from the François Vase, 6th cent.* B.C. *Archaeological Museum, Florence.*

This is the mythical story of Minos' family at Knossos, as preserved by ancient tradition. Homer and Hesiod, Herodotus and Thucydides, Bacchylides, Pindar, Plutarch, Diodorus Siculus and others give us details and variations of the same myth as well as other stories about Minos and information about the history of Crete. Homer in the *Iliad*, for example, in the list of ships which took part in the Trojan expedition, mentions that Crete sent eighty ships under the command of King Idomeneus of Knossos, grandson of Minos. The historian Herodotus tells us of an expedition of Cretans which accompanied or followed Minos when he pursued Daidalos to Sicily. It was a large expedition in which all the cities of Crete participated, with the exception of Polichne and Praisos. In order to avenge Minos' death they disembarked at Minoa and besieged Kamikos, but to no avail. On their return they were hampered by a great tempest to the south-east of Italy and so remained in the West, where they founded the colony of Hyria. Crete was deserted and received new inhabitants, including some Greeks. Later it was depopulated a second time, after the Trojan War, as a result of plague and famine.

Diodorus Siculus, a historian of the first century B.C., refers to Minos' death in Sicily and describes the king's tomb at Minoa, furnishing the detail that Theron — tyrant of Akragas in Sicily in the 5th century — found Minos' bones and sent them back to Crete for reinterment there.

It seems clear from a study of ancient tradition that even as early as the 8th century, when the Homeric epics were composed, the ancient Greeks believed implicitly in the important historical role of Crete and, in general outline, held the following view. The autochthonous population of Crete was made up of Kydonians and Eteocretans. Their king was Asterios, who married the oriental princess Europa and so founded the dynasty which boasted its descent from Zeus himself. The Cretans were lords of the seas; they founded colonies in the isles of the Aegean and travelled far to the east and west. However, earthquakes came, the fleet was destroyed off Italy and Crete was laid waste. Greeks emigrated to Crete, but not all its original inhabitants had disappeared. The Kydonians withdrew to the west and the Eteocretans to the eastern part of the island. By the time of Minos' grandson, Idomeneus, Crete had recovered sufficiently to send eighty ships to Troy, no mean force when compared with the hundred ships despatched by Agamemnon, king of Mycenae, and the ninety which accompanied Nestor, king of Pylos. After the Trojan War Crete was again denuded of its population and resettled by new migrants, some of them Dorians.

This was the picture which the ancient Greeks had of Minoan Crete, as is apparent from the myths, and the modern historian may succumb to the great temptation to correlate the myths concerning the colonies of Minos with the archaeological finds on the islands of Thera, Kea, Melos, Rhodes, etc., where there is evidence of marked Minoan influence. Similarly, on reading Herodotus' account of the two occasions when Crete was depopulated, one is tempted to ponder over the corresponding archaeological evidence of disasters: one in the years of the great heyday of the Minoan civilisation, which seems to have been followed by the settlement of

Mycenaeans at Knossos, and the other following the Trojan War. However, these correlations, though attractive, are dangerous, because there is no way of knowing which elements of the myth represent historical reality and which are products of the authors' imagination. It may well be true that the heroes lived in Crete in the prehistoric period, but their exploits were written down centuries later in historical times, when the Crete of mythology was influenced by the civilisation of the era of the author who has bequeathed us the myth. Myth is never history, and a knowledge of myth is no more than an aid to the study of ancient civilisation. In any case, what do the various versions of the same myth conceal? Why is Ariadne's fate different in different versions? In one she is abandoned by Theseus on Naxos and hangs herself from a tree, in another she marries Dionysos, in another she is killed by Artemis on the island of Dia, and there are still more versions of her death. No other heroine of a myth is represented as dying in so many different ways, and therefore the myth may perhaps be interpreted on the basis of the religious beliefs of the Minoans. Ariadne would then be identified with the goddess of vegetation, who dies each year to be reborn later, in the spring.

What, then, are the facts behind each myth? Behind the pre-Hellenic word *labyrinthos* — which is etymologically allied to the word *labrys* (double axe) — is perhaps the very palace of Knossos, the ruins of which reveal the labyrinthine complexity of its structure. Surely it would have inspired awe in its contemporaries and so, probably, later generations devised the myth of the Labyrinth built by the renowned Daidalos. Incised double axes have been found on the walls of the palace and the double axe, which is believed to have been used for sacrificing the bull in Minoan times, was one of the religious symbols of the Cretans. The mythical story of the youths devoured by the Minotaur perhaps echoes the sport of bull-games *(taurokathapsia),* much beloved by the Minoans, in which boys and girls performed dangerous acrobatics upon the bulls. We have copious illustrations of this sport in Minoan art. Professor J.W. Graham has suggested that the sport was held in the Central Court of the palace, that is within the mythical Labyrinth. And perhaps the name of Europa is not unrelated to the fact that the civilisation which bears the name of her son, Minos, was the first advanced European civilisation.

There are also other myths about Minos' family. One of these refers to his son, Glaukos, who as a small boy wandered about the palace cellars and was eventually drowned in a huge jar of honey. He was found there through the prophetic abilities of Polyidos, whom Minos then ordered to bring his son back to life and so incarcerated him in a vaulted chamber with Glaukos' body. Polyidos saw a snake in there and killed it. Quite soon, however, he noticed another snake approach the dead one, go away and then come back with a plant in its mouth, which it rubbed on the body of the dead snake and immediately revived it. In jubilation Polyidos resurrected Glaukos with the same plant. But Minos also demanded that he initiate his son in the secrets of the art of prophecy. Polyidos obeyed, but before he departed on his ship he asked Glaukos to spit into his mouth.

Glaukos did so and immediately lost his power of prophecy.

We conclude with Minos himself, king of Knossos. We do not know whether only one king of that name existed, who renewed his sovereignty every nine years in conference with Zeus, or whether Minos was a title having the same meaning as Pharaoh had for the Egyptians or, in more recent times, Tsar for the Russians: that is, whether it was merely the title of the king at Knossos. What is certain is that for the ancient Greeks he was the worthy, just but easily angered ruler of the Cretans in the prehistoric era and, above all, that he enjoyed maritime supremacy in the Aegean.

HISTORY OF THE EXCAVATIONS

When Robert Pashley described the site he believed to be Knossos in his book *Travels in Crete* (1837), he mentioned masses of Roman bricks as the only ancient remains. The palace of Knossos was invisible, buried beneath the earth. There was a village near by, Makrytichos, so named after the remains of Roman ramparts which had survived in the area. However, even if Minoan Knossos had, with the passage of the centuries, been lost from human view, it had not been lost from human memory. The myths of Theseus and Ariadne and the terrible Minotaur were always great favourites and interest in the dark Labyrinth was particularly lively. So in the 17th century W. Lithgow wrote in his book *The Totall Discourse* that while in Crete he was shown the entrance to Daidalos' Labyrinth, which he describes. What he actually saw, however, was the way into the ancient quarries located in the vicinity of Gortyn.

There is a strange tale about the discovery of part of the palace of Knossos in the days of the Roman Emperor Nero. It is recorded in the preface of a forged literary work of the 3rd century A.D. known as the Chronicles of Dictys, which purported to be an eye-witness account of the Trojan War. The story goes that in the thirteenth year of Nero's reign there was an earthquake in Crete, which brought to light some tombs at Knossos. In them a shepherd found a tin box containing pieces of bark with curious writing on them. The scholars sent by Nero recognised the characters as Phoenician and translated them, and the text which emerged from the translation was the Chronicles of Dictys. This tale brings to mind the inscribed clay tablets found in Evans' excavation of the West Magazines of the palace.

The history of excavations in the Aegean region begins in 1870 when Heinrich Schliemann, a wealthy self-made German merchant and fanatical believer in the historical value of Homer, set off, *Iliad* in hand, to discover Troy. He excavated the mound of Hissarlik in Asia Minor and actually found the site of Troy, though he was erroneous in the dating of his finds. In 1876 he came to Mycenae, where he unearthed the rich Mycenaean tombs and declared that he had found the corpse of Agamemnon himself with his gold face mask. Even though the skeleton was not that of the king

8. Sir Arthur John Evans, the English archaeologist who excavated the palace of Knossos and brought to light a lost civilisation which he named Minoan after the mythical king of Knossos.

but only a distant ancestor, there was a great surge of interest in the world of Homer, which had been shown to be not entirely fictitious. Homer's cities of Troy and Mycenae had been identified. Why not Knossos?

In 1878, two years after the commencement of Schliemann's excavations at Mycenae, another merchant and antiquarian, the Greek Minos Kalokairinos, struck his pick into the hill of Kephala near his native Herakleion and brought to light the storerooms of a building which he immediately identified as the palace of his namesake, the king of Crete. These were a few of the extensive magazines which were later uncovered in the West Wing of the palace. Twelve *pithoi* (storage jars) and other smaller vases and sherds were found. At the same time the Society for the Promotion of Learning was founded in Herakleion with Joseph Hazzidakis and Stephanos Xanthoudides as enthusiastic members of its governing body. One of the Society's aims was archaeological investigation and the establishment of a collection of antiquities in Herakleion.

Minos Kalokairinos' excavations were stopped by the Turkish Governor of Crete. Then the American journalist W.J. Stillman, former American Consul in Crete, conceived the novel idea that the building at Knossos might be the Labyrinth of Greek mythology. He wanted to continue the excavations on the hill of Kephala, but he too was soon stopped by the Turks. Stillman's articles on Knossos were read by many people with interest and Schliemann decided to complete his archaeological research into the world of Homer by digging at Knossos as well. So he came to Crete and began negotiating for the purchase of the site from its Turkish owners, but without success. It is said the deal broke down because of a few olive trees, for when Schliemann counted the olive trees on the plot he had agreed to buy, he found 889 instead of the 2,500 he had been told were there. Businessman that he was, he was furious and cancelled the purchase. Then in 1894 Arthur Evans came to Crete. He it was who was destined to excavate, study and publish the palace of Knossos and through his work to lay the foundations of research into another, pre-Mycenaean, civilisation which he called Minoan after the name of the king of Knossos.

Arthur Evans was born into a prosperous and educated English family in 1851 and studied at Oxford. As a young man he travelled as correspondent of the *Manchester Guardian* in the Balkans and supported the liberation movements of the peoples of the Balkan peninsula, on one occasion being imprisoned by the Austrians at Ragusa. He returned to Oxford, where, at the age of 31, he became Keeper of the Ashmolean Museum. He had a passion for archaeology, especially prehistoric scripts. He studied the sealstones which Schliemann had found at Mycenae and was convinced that a civilisation such as the Mycenaean must have had a system of writing. The sealstones are small objects, round, ovoid or prismatic in shape, made of semi-precious stones or ivory. It was apparent that they were used as seals because of the designs on them, which sometimes resemble a kind of hieroglyphic script like that of Egypt. Because Evans wanted to study the unknown script of the sealstones he started collecting them. He found some, similar to the Mycenaean ones, in an Athens antique shop and was informed that they were of Cretan provenance, so in 1894 he went to Crete, where he collected several more. He published his study of these objects in *Cretan Pictographs and Pre-Phoenician Scripts* in 1895, and at the same time his travels in Crete awakened his general interest in the antiquities on the island. He visited the hill of Kephala at Knossos, which was still virtually intact except for the trial trenches dug by the Cretan M. Kalokairinos. In her biography of Arthur Evans *(Time and Chance)* his half-sister, Joan Evans, has some excerpts from his diary recording his impressions on his first visit to Knossos.

Evans began negotiating to buy the site from its owners with the help of

Hazzidakis. With his own money he bought part of the site, but there he had to stop on account of the excessive demands of the other owners. Furthermore, the political situation on the island, with the uprisings of the Cretans and the Turkish reprisals, was not favourable. However, when Crete was declared an autonomous state in 1898, with Prince George of the Hellenes as Governor General, the situation changed. In 1899, following moves by J. Hazzidakis and S. Xanthoudides, an archaeological law was drafted for the first time in Crete and the necessary preconditions for the excavation of Knossos were established. The purchase of the archaeological site was completed and on March 23rd, 1900, the new systematic excavations at Knossos commenced, financed mainly by Evans himself. Almost from the beginning his colleagues included Duncan Mackenzie, who had previously participated in the excavations at Phylakopi on Melos, the architect Theodore Fyfe and the painter E. Gilliéron (père).

At the start of the excavations there were thirty workers, but their number soon rose to over a hundred and the work proceeded at a very rapid pace. After only five days Evans had enough evidence at his disposal to realise that the large building which was coming to light belonged to a civilisation older than the Mycenaean. On the seventh day he found the first clay tablet with traces of script on it, on April 13th the throne of Minos was discovered and on April 15th Evans wrote to his father that he had unearthed a large number of clay tablets similar to those found at Babylon but inscribed with the prehistoric script of the Cretans. His interest in the script was being rewarded and, at the same time, the whole civilisation to which it belonged was being revealed. So by the close of the first year (1900) the whole of the West Wing had been excavated and in the following year he began digging the East Wing. Within two years the Throne Room, the Central Court, the Grand Staircase, the Magazines and the Domestic Quarters had been revealed. By the end of the third season of excavation (late 1902) almost all of the palace had been uncovered. There followed supplementary excavations inside the palace and explorations outside it, which ended in the discovery of the houses of palace officials, the Royal Road, the Little Palace, the Tomb of Isopata, etc.

In 1914 the First World War stopped work, which was not resumed until 1922. It then continued for a further ten years until 1932. To the initial collaborators others were added, such as Piet de Jong the architect, E. Gilliéron (fils) the painter and the archaeologists E.J. Forsdyke and J.D.S. Pendlebury. Evans published his discoveries between 1920 and 1935 in his great four-volume work *The Palace of Minos at Knossos* (plus a volume for the index). In 1935 he was present at the unveiling of his bust in bronze, which was erected at the entrance to the site of Knossos. He died in 1941, aged 90, at Youlbury in England, having dedicated fifty long years to research into the Minoan civilisation. Some of his views have been disputed, needless to say, by recent scholars — this is inevitable, and quite right and proper, as scholarship progresses — but his pioneering work made an immense contribution to archaeology which has proved fundamental.

MINOANS AND KNOSSOS

Before visiting Knossos it is essential to have some knowledge of its history. What one sees today are but the ruins of the palace and the nearby residences of its officials. The settlement of Knossos, however, was in existence before the palace was built; the site was already inhabited by the end of the 7th millennium B.C., that is at the beginning of the **Neolithic.** This period is characterised by a productive economy: men were not merely food-gatherers as they had been of old, but began producing their own food by cultivation and animal husbandry. They settled in one place, used carefully-worked stone tools and began to manufacture vases of pottery. All these features distinguish the Neolithic from the earlier Palaeolithic and Mesolithic eras. It is of considerable interest that the oldest Neolithic remains found so far in Crete come from Knossos.

Excavations carried out by the British School of Archaeology under the Central Court of the palace have revealed the Neolithic settlement down to 7 metres below the surface, the great depth being due to successive habitations. Each stage of occupation constituted a separate stratum. The excavations revealed ten building levels in all, the lowest of which is, naturally, the earliest. In this early layer we find remains of the first settlement at Knossos, which was probably semi-permanent in character, with temporary huts. However, there is definite evidence of the cultivation of cereals and of animal husbandry, although pottery is completely lacking. Consequently we have here a Preceramic phase of the Neolithic. In the ensuing levels which belong to the Neolithic proper (Early, Middle and Late), there is a sudden appearance of dwellings with stone socles and mud-brick superstructure, developed pottery and even examples of modelling. The settlement seems to have been large, covering an area roughly equal to that of the later palace of Knossos, and later even larger. Around 3800 B.C. Neolithic settlements appeared in other parts of Crete too (Katsambas, Gortyn), while from circa 3500 onwards, that is in the Late Neolithic, a great expansion of population is observed throughout the entire island. At Knossos the Neolithic strata succeeded one another and by now it had a population estimated at between one and two thousand. Who the Neolithic inhabitants of Crete were we do not know. Throughout the long Neolithic era the culture seems to have evolved without interruption. Some scholars believe that the population of Preceramic Knossos was of Aegean origin, while others maintain that the people of the Neolithic

◄ *9. Sir Arthur Evans (in the white suit), Duncan Mackenzie and Theodore Fyfe with some of the excavation workmen, photographed during the course of restoration work on the Grand Staircase of the palace. (Courtesy of the Ashmolean Museum, Oxford)*

10. A Minoan woman as depicted in the Dancing Girl Fresco from the Queen's Hall in the palace of Knossos. Herakleion Museum.

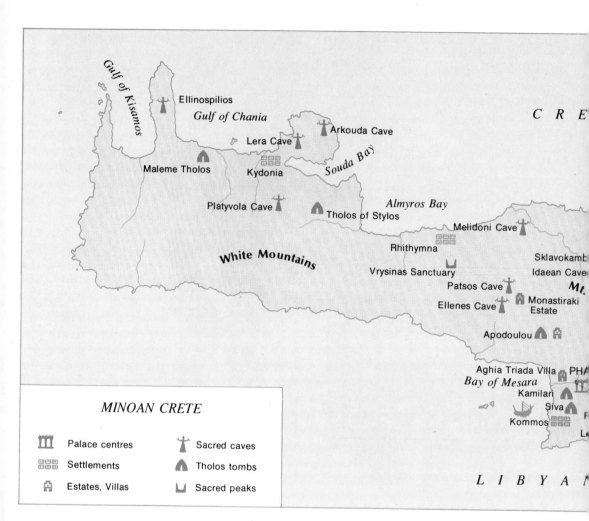

CRE

Gulf of Kisamos

Gulf of Chania

Ellinospilios

Arkouda Cave

Lera Cave

Souda Bay

Maleme Tholos

Kydonia

Almyros Bay

Platyvola Cave

Tholos of Stylos

Melidoni Cave

Rhithymna

Sklavokamb

White Mountains

Idaean Cave

Vrysinas Sanctuary

Patsos Cave

Mt.

Ellenes Cave

Monastiraki
Estate

Apodoulou

Aghia Triada Villa

PHA

Bay of Mesara

Kamilari

Siva

Kommos

L I B Y A N

MINOAN CRETE

▥ Palace centres		⚚ Sacred caves
▦ Settlements		⏶ Tholos tombs
⌂ Estates, Villas		⊔ Sacred peaks

26

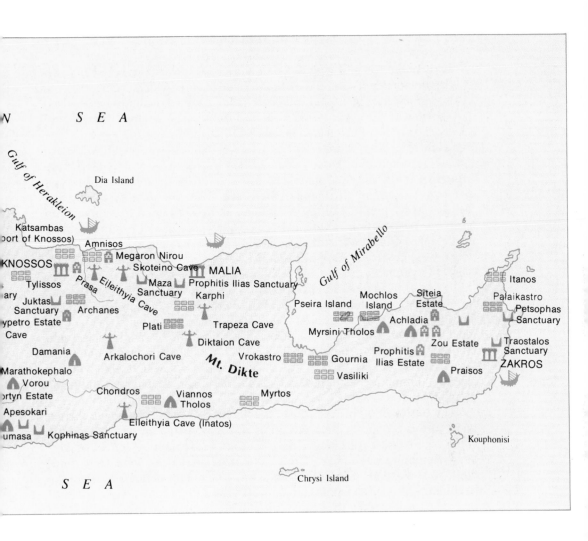

N   S E A

Gulf of Herakleion

Dia Island

Katsambas
(port of Knossos)
Amnisos
Megaron Nirou
KNOSSOS
Skoteino Cave   MALIA
Tylissos   Prasa   Eileithyia Cave
Maza   Prophitis Ilias Sanctuary
...ary   Sanctuary   Karphi
Juktas   Sanctuary   Archanes
...ypetro Estate
Cave   Plati
Damania   Arkalochori Cave   Vrokastro
Marathokephalo   Mt. Dikte
Vorou
...rtyn Estate   Chondros   Viannos   Myrtos
Apesokari   Tholos
...umasa   Kophinas Sanctuary   Eileithyia Cave (Inatos)

Trapeza Cave
Diktaion Cave

Gulf of Mirabello

Pseira Island   Mochlos Island   Siteia Estate   Itanos
Myrsini Tholos   Achladia   Palaikastro
Gournia   Prophitis Ilias Estate   Zou Estate   Petsophas Sanctuary
Vasiliki   Praisos   Traostalos Sanctuary
ZAKROS

Kouphonisi

S E A

Chrysi Island

11. *Map of Crete showing important Minoan sites. So far the existence of four palaces has been established with certainty, all of them situated on strategically placed sites controlling plains and with access to the sea. In the heyday of the Minoan civilisation palatial villas and country mansions were built, while towns and villages grew up either around the palaces or on other carefully selected sites, often near a harbour or in close proximity to major sea routes. The Minoans practised their religion at sanctuaries of several different kinds: the map shows most of the peak sanctuaries and sacred caves. The dead were buried in graves of various types, the most imposing being the tholos or "beehive" tombs, which remained in use, with certain modifications of design as time went on, from the beginning of the Bronze Age until after the end of the Minoan period.*

period came in small groups from Asia Minor, in primitive boats via the Dodecanese.

Early in the 3rd millennium (some time between 2800 and 2600) a new era commenced in Crete. This was the **Bronze Age,** which is characterised by the introduction of copper followed in due course by a more generalised use of metals. The transition from the Stone Age to the Bronze Age occurred gradually during the course of a brief interim period known as the Sub-Neolithic. The Bronze Age in Crete coincides with the flowering of the civilisation which Evans named Minoan: that is why it is called the **Minoan Period** and the inhabitants of Crete are referred to as Minoans, although this was not the name of their race. Who were the Minoans? The fact that many features of the Neolithic culture continued to evolve even after the introduction of metal-working indicates that the old Neolithic inhabitants constituted a basic element of the Bronze Age population, which was, however, reinforced at intervals by new groups of immigrants who most probably came from Anatolia (and perhaps a few from Africa, the Proto-Libyans as Evans called them). These immigrants spread throughout Crete and mixed peacefully with the indigenous population. We know of the Minoans from their wall-paintings, in which we see an idealised picture of them, and from their magnificent architectural and engineering works. Anthropologically they are classified as belonging to the "Mediterranean race", the characteristics of which are dolicho-cephaly, diminutive stature, dark eyes and dark hair. Brachycephalic skulls are comparatively rare.

The introduction of bronze and the practice of metallurgy gave a great boost to the economy. Arts and crafts developed steadily. The Neolithic communities were succeeded by pre-urban settlements, such as Myrtos near Hierapetra in southern Crete, and large structures were sometimes built, as at Vasiliki, also near Hierapetra, which may perhaps indicate the beginnings of centralised government. It seems that society was organised into clans, to judge by the large multiple tholos tombs of the Mesara Plain in southern Crete.

Pottery, seal-stone carving, metal-working and goldsmithry flourished. At the same time, the quest for sources of copper (Cyprus) and tin (Asia Minor) for the manufacture of bronze, an alloy which is more durable than copper, encouraged the development of seafaring and commerce. The Cretans forged international relations, particularly with the Cyclades, and are thought to have established a colony on the island of Kythera, south of the Peloponnese. The number of known settlements already in existence in Crete by ca. 2000 B.C. comes to over a hundred and the island's population is estimated to have been approximately 75,000. One of these settlements was Knossos, of course, but the site has very few remains from this period because the building layers in question were razed when the hilltop was levelled for the construction of the palace, with the result that the Neolithic building levels are now immediately below the floor of the Central Court of the palace.

The combination of the Neolithic farming economy with the technological specialisation brought about by the introduction of metals laid the foundations for the great economic and political development of Crete at the beginning of the 2nd millennium B.C. So, in about 1900, a major change took place in Crete through the continued evolution of elements from the preceding period: the first palaces were built at Knossos, Phaistos, Malia and Zakros, all on important sites controlling plains and with access to the sea. At the same time the first real towns grew up around the palaces as well as on other sites, such as low hillocks near a harbour or in close proximity to major sea routes. The founding of the palaces implies a concentration of power in the hands of kings who controlled agricultural and industrial production as well as trade. The palaces are complex buildings with large magazines for storing such produce as cereals, wine, oil, etc., workshops in which craftsmen produced works of art for the needs of the palace and for export, shrines, priests' quarters and, finally, royal apartments, reception rooms and places for staging spectacles. The palaces were political, economic and religious centres. That of Knossos is the largest and most important, and so the king of Knossos may perhaps have enjoyed some sort of suzerainty over the kings of the other palaces. The palaces and towns were evidently unfortified, which points to the absence of external dangers (perhaps thanks to the might of the navy) and also to the peaceful coexistence of the various palatial centres in Crete, without mutual rivalry. More attention was given to the promotion of the arts, especially architecture and pottery. In this period the fast potter's wheel was in use for the manufacture of vases in elaborate shapes, characterised by polychrome decoration on a black background and torsion of the motifs. This is the so-called Kamares ware, named after the cave of Kamares on Mt. Ida where such vases were first found. Imported Kamares ware found in Egypt and Syria and evidence of Minoan influence at Phylakopi on Melos testify to the great expansion of trade in these times. In general, the founding of the palaces was accompanied by a greater degree of cultural homogeneity with centralised organisation and strong government, and this concentration of power created a hierarchy of classes headed by the king. At the same time an organised system of writing was developed, essential for the bureaucratic control of production. Initially it was a hieroglyphic script, but it was later simplified into the so-called Linear A system.

Unfortunately very little now remains of the palaces and towns of this period, because the later palaces and towns were built on the very same sites. The old palace of Knossos (like the others) had more or less the same form as the later palace, the ruins of which are visible today. The town spread out around the palace, and on the hills of Prophitis Ilias and Monastiriako Kephali (or Acropolis) were the cemeteries with tombs that foreshadowed the later chamber tombs (these were natural caves and hollows which were artificially enlarged), while on the hill of Gypsades a tholos tomb was built in those times. The first palace of Knossos was badly damaged twice (probably by earthquakes) and was repaired both times. In 1700, however, it was completely destroyed, as were the other palaces at about the same time. The view that these disasters were due to invasion by a foreign people such as the Luwians from south-western Anatolia or the Hyksos from Egypt does not seem to be valid, for there is no apparent break in the evolution of the civilisation. It is more likely that the destruction was caused by severe earthquakes.

After the disaster of 1700 B.C. large-scale construction works were put in hand on Crete. The palaces were completely rebuilt after the ruins of the earlier buildings had been levelled and covered over, the new palaces being the ones which have survived to this day, with additions and alterations made after another disaster in about 1600. In general there was an increase in population and considerable building activity both in the coastal towns, such as Gournia, Mochlos, Palaikastro and on the island of Pseira, and in the towns centred round the large palaces. Smaller palatial villas were built at Archanes, Aghia Triada and elsewhere, while at the same time a new kind of establishment, the country mansion, appeared in considerable numbers throughout the countryside. The country mansions were large buildings with installations related to the agricultural economy and local craft industries and were most probably the residences of the local overlord of each district, who was a vassal of the king in the large palace and responsible to him for controlling local production. Thus a form of feudalism came into being in the economic system. The social system was still based on a class hierarchy headed by the king. Besides the priests, public officials, nobles, farmers and stockbreeders, there was a class of merchants and mariners, and there must also have been a class of scribes, because writing was widely practised in this period: specimens of Linear A script have so far been found at no less than 27 Minoan sites. In art, apart from the splendid achievements in pottery, metallurgy and glyptics, great advances were made in another sphere, that of wall-painting. Not only the palaces, but country villas and even town houses too, were embellished with magnificent wall-paintings depicting scenes from everyday life, religion and nature. Furthermore, it was in the period of the new palaces that the expansion of Minoan influence abroad was at its greatest. In addition to the trade with Egypt and the Levant, there is evidence of pronounced Minoan influence or Minoan settlements at a great many sites in the south Aegean, including the islands of Kythera, Kea, Paros, Naxos, Melos, Thera, Rhodes, Kos and Karpathos and the cities of Miletos and Iasos in Asia Minor. These form a zone of Minoan influence facing the north coast of Crete along the whole length of the island. Minoan cultural elements also appear in the Peloponnese (Messenia and Mycenae).

At Knossos the palace was surrounded by a city which in those days reached as far as the hills of Gypsades and Acropolis, with a population estimated by Evans at about 80,000. Very few parts of this city have been excavated.

Among the buildings erected during this period are the houses in the environs of the palace, which in all probability belonged to officials and

12, 13. Faience plaques found in the excavations at the palace of Knossos, showing what Minoan houses looked like. Herakleion Museum.

BLUE GUIDE
CRETE

Blue Guide Crete
Paolo Pugsley
Somerset Books, 2010, 432pp
416 colour and 15 b/w illus
Paperback, £14.95

pub/
histo
a co
subj
of th
7-25
of th
Neol
fascii
Age
tices
matu
Class
and la
BC–A
reade
(1204
1898)

Abc
Minoa
guide
on thi
tion o
Bronze
taxing
echoec
inside
ologica
in wha
one mi

Crete is so acknowledged as an archaeological

members of the priesthood, and the so-called "Little Palace" of Knossos, which stood to the north-west of the large palace and communicated with it via the "Royal Road". Notable houses lined the road on both sides, while to the south of the palace, near the Minoan viaduct over the Vlychia stream, stood a building (the Caravanserai), which was probably a guest-house for visitors to the palace. The large royal tomb of Isopata, the tholos tomb of Kephala and the Temple Tomb, a monumental funerary structure to the south of the palace, were also built during this period.

After two partial destructions, one in 1600 and one in 1500 B.C., the palaces were totally destroyed in 1450 and were never rebuilt. So the period of the New Palaces, which lasted for two and a half centuries and constituted the "Golden Age" of Minoan civilisation, came to an end. All the Minoan centres — palaces, villas, country mansions and towns — were destroyed, many of them by fire, and abandoned. The palace of Knossos was the exception, in that it survived the great catastrophe. What was the cause of this multiple disaster? Was it the eruption of the Thera volcano, which destroyed the settlement of Akrotiri and submerged the greater part of the island of Thera beneath the sea, creating a huge caldera and generating earthquakes, tidal waves and a fall-out of volcanic tephra on Crete, among other places? Were the Mycenaeans who conquered Crete responsible for the havoc, or did they perhaps exploit the disastrous con-sequences of the earthquakes and seize the opportunity of settling on the once mighty island? Each school of thought has its supporters but also its weak points. Certainly life at the palace of Knossos continued, and after some time the sites of Phaistos, Malia, Aghia Triada, Tylissos, Gournia and Palaikastro were reoccupied to some extent. In the fifty-year period following the 1450 disaster two features of note are apparent. The first was the recession of Minoan influence abroad and its eventual replacement by the Mycenaean presence. The second is that Mycenaeans actually settled in Crete itself, at the palace of Knossos. Indications of this are to be found in cultural changes — in the arts, the manner of burial, the militaristic spirit which now appears for the first time, and so on. Proof, however, is fur-nished by the clay tablets of this period found in the palace of Knossos: they are written in another script, Linear B, which seems to be a modifica-tion of the older Linear A system. Linear B tablets have been found in Mycenaean centres in Greece and their language is Mycenaean Greek, but the language of the Linear A tablets, believed to be Minoan, remains a mystery. The Knossos tablets mention the names of 85 Cretan settlements and show that the Mycenaeans of Knossos exercised a degree of control over the rest of the island. However, despite the Mycenaean elements, the cultural base continued to be Minoan even after the palace of Knossos was finally destroyed by fire a little later than 1400 B.C. (round about 1375) due

14. The founding of the palaces implies a concentration of power in the hands of kings. The famous gypsum throne illustrated here, found by Evans in situ in the Throne Room of the palace of Knossos, is probably the oldest known throne in Europe.

to some unknown cause which may have been earthquake, insurrection of the Minoan population or conflict between the Mycenaeans at Knossos and the Mycenaeans of the Greek mainland. The palace was not rebuilt this time and it was not until the 13th century that the site was reoccupied. Evidence of this resettlement is provided by the Shrine of the Double Axes in the South-East Sector, the alterations in the area of the North Entrance, the storing of pithoi by the South Propylaeum and other changes. Parts of the Little Palace and the "Unexplored Mansion" next to it were also reoccupied. These habitations have caused some scholars to suggest that the palace was not destroyed until after 1200, which would explain the similarity between the Linear B tablets of Knossos and those from Pylos in the Peloponnese, which are dated to 1200. This view has not yet gained majority acceptance among archaeologists, its chief exponent being Professor L.R. Palmer.

After the destruction of the palace in about 1375 the city of Knossos continued to be inhabited, as is evident from the cemeteries in the surrounding area (Zapher Papoura, Sellopoulo, Gypsades). Life also went on at other old settlements such as Amnisos, Tylissos, Phaistos, Aghia Triada and Malia, and new ones were founded at Kephali Chondrou, Aghia Pelaghia, Gournes, Damania and elsewhere. In western Crete, at Chania, there is evidence of increased prosperity, and perhaps there was a shift of power from Knossos to Kydonia (the modern Chania), where there was probably a palace and close contacts were maintained with the Peloponnese. Around 1200 B.C. some settlements were abandoned while others, such as Kephali Chondrou, were destroyed, and it may be that a fresh wave of Mycenaeans came to Crete after the disasters on the Greek mainland. During the 12th century settlements in low-lying areas were abandoned and others were built in places difficult of access, such as Kastri above Palaikastro and Karphi above the plateau of Lasithi. All these are signs of upheaval and population movement to avoid danger. Finally, non-Minoan cultural elements were introduced, such as cremation of the dead, the use of fibulae and pins on women's clothes, which indicate a change in the type of dress, and the gradual spread of iron. This is the **Sub-Minoan** phase, after which Crete enters the so-called historical era, the **Iron Age.**

Thus ended the period of Minoan civilisation in Crete. In order to study a period it is essential to have a system of chronology. This is achieved in two ways, each of which complements the other: relative dating and absolute dating. Relative dating is based on the succession of different periods: on the evidence of the stratigraphy, and aided by the development of pottery, the archaeologists decide which find is earlier and which later. Absolute dating determines the exact starting and finishing dates of each period. The excavator of Knossos, Evans, working in collaboration with Mackenzie and basing his conclusions on pottery development, divided the Minoan era into three major periods: **Early Minoan (EM), Middle Minoan (MM)** and **Late Minoan (LM).** Each period was divided into three sub-periods, I, II and III, and each of these into phases (usually two, A and

15. *All the Cretan palaces had large store-rooms for grain, wine, oil and other commodities. This photograph shows the West Magazines of the palace of Knossos, with part of the West Court behind.*

B). This system of relative chronology is still used today, though in conjunction with a newer system propounded in 1958 by the archaeologist Nikolaos Platon, who later excavated the palace of Zakros. The disadvantage of Evans' system is that it is primarily based on pottery development; frequently, however, a pottery style in one part of Crete could coexist with an earlier one in another part of the island. For this reason it is not always clear when, for example, we speak of LM IA and LM IB whether we are speaking about two successive periods of time or two different pottery styles. Platon's system is based on the historical turning-points marked by the successive destructions of the palatial centres. Thus the Minoan era is divided into four periods: **Prepalatial** (from the introduction of copper until the founding of the palaces, coinciding with Evans' EM and MM IA),

Protopalatial (the period of the first palaces in Crete, coinciding with Evans' MM IB and MM II), **Neopalatial** (the period of the new palaces, coinciding with Evans' MM III, LM I to LM IIIA₁) and **Postpalatial** (the period after the final destruction of the palace of Knossos, coinciding with Evans' LM IIIA₂, B and C). Each of these periods is subdivided into three or more phases, separated by the intervening minor destructions of the palaces.

The absolute dating of the Minoan world was begun by Evans and continued by other scholars. It is based mainly on relations with Egypt, where the chronology of cultural development is known thanks to the surviving inscriptions on ancient Egyptian monuments. The system relies on the evidence of dated Egyptian objects found at Minoan sites and, conversely, Minoan artefacts found in Egyptian contexts of known date. The period of the first palaces, for example, is found to be contemporary with the 12th and 13th dynasties in Egypt, as proved by Egyptian scarabs at Knossos and MM I and MM II pottery in Egypt.

Through the combined use of relative and absolute dating, the chronological system for the Minoan world works out approximately as follows:

Prepalatial Period   2600 - 1900 B.C.
Protopalatial Period 1900 - 1700 B.C.
Neopalatial Period   1700 - 1400 B.C.
Postpalatial Period   1400 - 1100 B.C.

After the end of the Minoan era, in historic times, the city of Knossos retained its prehistoric name. In the Geometric period it was already flourishing again, as is evident from the nearby cemetery of Fortetsa, while in the Archaic period there is evidence of the cult of Demeter on the hill of Gypsades, where there was a temple in the Classical period too. It seems that in Classical times the town lay to the north of the palace site. Knossos was one of the first cities in Crete to mint silver coinage; traditional subjects were used, such as the Labyrinth and the Minotaur. As a city-state it was a member of the Cretan *Koinon* (a fairly free association of Cretan cities) during the Hellenistic period, but it was also involved in incessant local conflict. From 221-219 B.C. Knossos, together with the city of Gortyn, controlled the whole of Crete after sacking the neighbouring city of Lyttos. Thereafter, sometimes in collaboration with Gortyn, sometimes at war with it, it maintained its pre-eminence until the conquest of Crete by the Romans in 67 B.C., when Gortyn rose to supremacy. A Roman colony known as *Colonia Julia Nobilis* was established at Knossos. The Roman city was large and a villa built in Hadrian's reign, the so-called Villa Dionysus, still survives. In Byzantine times Knossos was a Bishop's see and there are remains of a 6th-century basilica in the vicinity. After the Arab conquest of Crete the port of Herakleion began to grow in importance and it developed steadily thereafter, while Knossos vanished into oblivion until 1878, when Minos Kalokairinos' pickaxe brought it to light.

16, 17. *The bureaucratic control of production necessitated an organised system of writing, which in the Minoan world was a syllabic script of one form or another. Initially a hieroglyphic script (16, left) was used; then, during the period when the Minoan civilisation was at its zenith, the script known as Linear A (16, right) was introduced; and finally, in the so-called period of the Mycenaean dynasty, a new linear script known as Linear B (17) came into use. The last of these was deciphered by Michael Ventris, an English architect, who found that the language of the Linear B tablets was Greek.*

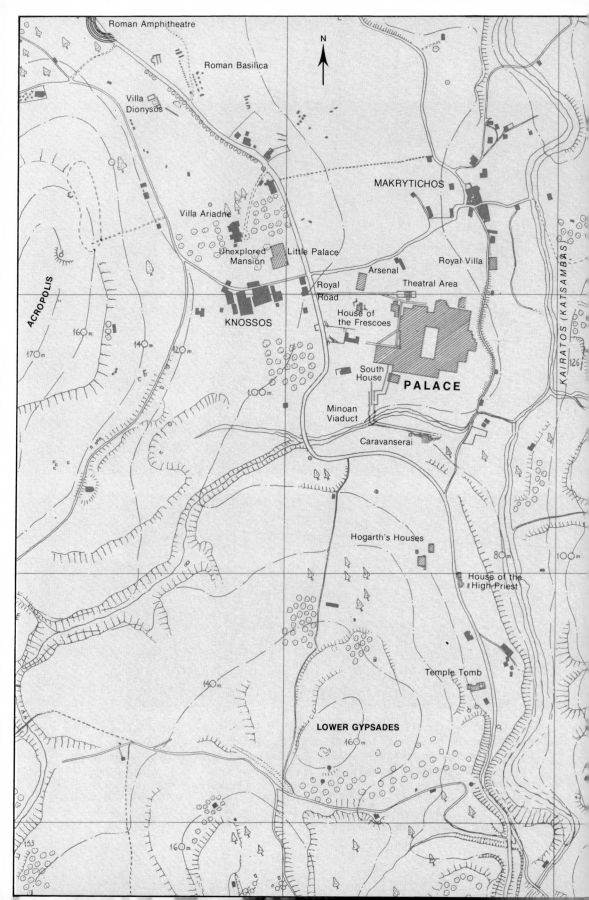

THE ARCHAEOLOGICAL SITE

ROUTE FROM HERAKLEION TO KNOSSOS

Knossos is situated five kilometres away from Herakleion in the valley of the Katsambas river, on its west bank. To the east of Knossos rises the hill of Prophitis Ilias, to the west the lower hill called Acropolis (or Monastiriako Kephali) and to the south the heights of Gypsades. To the north Knossos is hidden from the sea by the low hills at the ends of the two long ridges of Aghios Ioannis, which begins a little way beyond the Venizeleion Hospital, and Isopata, which begins at Zapher Papoura. The terrain here is composed of white sedimentary rock known as *kouskouras,* and because it is very soft it was very convenient for excavating tomb chambers in ancient times.

Minoan Knossos — the name is obviously pre-Hellenic — covered an area of approximately one square kilometre and had a population of about 80,000. With the palace as its centre it extended along the fertile valley as far as the neighbouring hills of Acropolis and Gypsades. Its cemeteries lay around it, on the heights of Isopata, Aghios Ioannis, Zapher Papoura, Sanatorium, Acropolis, Gypsades and Prophitis Ilias. Further north, on the coast, were its two harbours, one at the mouth of the Katsambas river (on the boundaries of the present town of Herakleion) and the other further east at Amnisos. There was a third harbour further east still, on the site of Nirou Chani.

In the Geometric and Archaic periods the site of the palace does not seem to have been inhabited (perhaps because it was regarded as sacred) and the city was shifted northwards. The sites of the Minoan cemeteries were reused and new necropoles were made. The classical and Roman city extended even further to the north and its cemeteries were again located on its northern outskirts. So the whole area between Herakleion and Knossos is full of remains of the Minoan, Geometric, Archaic, Classical, Roman and Christian periods. Buildings, walls, wells, assorted architectural members and, above all, tombs of all periods have been discovered and

18. Plan of the environs of the palace of Knossos (after S. Hood).

more are being found all the time.

Leave the centre of the city of Herakleion by the Knossos road. Some way off on the left, a short way out from the town centre, stands the hill of Isopata, where the **Royal Tomb of Isopata** was found. The tomb was destroyed in 1942 and nowadays we can only see what it looked like from books and Piet de Jong's restored view in the Herakleion Museum. It consisted of a rectangular masonry chamber roofed with a keel vault, approached by a rock-hewn dromos through an antechamber with niches along the sides, perhaps for objects connected with the cult of dead kings. The bodies were buried under the floor of the main chamber. Opposite the main entrance there was a blind doorway in the wall, perhaps for some purpose connected with religious beliefs. The tomb was built in LM IB but was much used in the LM II period (the so-called period of the Mycenaean dynasty at Knossos). It was described as a royal tomb partly because of its monumental construction and partly because of the finds of grave goods which had not been looted. To the north of the royal tomb a number of other tombs were found, one of them built of masonry and the others simply chamber tombs hewn from the rock.

The road continues through the suburb of **Aghios Ioannis,** where Late Minoan, Sub-Minoan and Protogeometric tombs have been found. After Aghios Ioannis you pass through another suburb, Ambelokipi (formerly known as **Chaniali Tekke** from the name of a private Turkish *tekke* in the neighbourhood). Here, besides two chamber tombs, excavators have discovered a tholos tomb which was in use from the Late Minoan until the end of the Orientalising period. The grave goods from this tomb, now on view in the Herakleion Museum, include Protogeometric and Geometric vases and a particularly splendid collection of jewellery, which was found inside two small vases buried in cavities to right and left of the entrance: a lovely crescent-shaped pendant of rock crystal, a necklace of chunky rock crystal beads, a gold fillet with a representation of a god taming a lion and many other fine pieces.

Continue as far as the Venizeleion Hospital (the old Sanatorium), passing on the way a turning to the right which leads to **Fortetsa.** Fortetsa is well-known on account of the great siege of Herakleion in the 17th century. When Herakleion was still under Venetian rule the Turks, who had previously subjugated Chania and Rethymnon, encamped at Fortetsa in 1648. So began the great siege of Herakleion, which was to last for 21 years until September 5th, 1669, when the garrison commander, Francesco Morosini, surrendered the town.

All along the Herakleion-Knossos road and in the whole area enclosed by Chaniali Tekke, the Venizeleion Hospital and Fortetsa, there was an extensive cemetery in the Geometric period, and others on the west slopes of the Acropolis hill. Some important tombs of the LM II period, known as the Warrior Graves on account of the weapons interred with the bodies, were discovered near the **Venizeleion Hospital.** Among the finds was the bronze helmet with cheek-pieces which is exhibited in the Herakleion Museum. Warrior graves have been found elsewhere in the Knossos region (Zapher Papoura): they testify to the new militaristic spirit indicating the presence of Mycenaean rulers at the palace of Knossos in the LM II period. In the same area, east of the hospital, Roman and Christian graves and an Early Christian church dating from the beginning of the 6th century have come to light. The church is a three-aisled basilica with a narthex opening into the central aisle. Mosaics with geometric designs and marble inlay adorned the floors. As is apparent from the finds, the region was initially a Roman cemetery and may also have served as a cemetery for the first Christians at Knossos. Later the church was built on top of the graves (perhaps in honour of the first Christians) and remained in use for many years, as is evident from the worn and repaired floors. No violent destruction took place, but the church gradually fell into disuse and was eventually abandoned, most probably in the 9th century.

A little further along the Herakleion-Knossos road, on the right, one can see some modern shed roofs and restored columns. These are the roofed ruins of a Roman villa, known as the **Villa Dionysos** after the Dionysiac themes of the mosaic floor dated to the 2nd century A.D. On the same site a large headless torso of the Emperor Hadrian was found. The villa has a central courtyard with three rooms on its north side, two rooms and a corridor or staircase on the south and the entrance to the main room of the house on the west. There was a peristyle of Doric limestone columns around the courtyard and Corinthian marble columns at the entrance to the west room. All the rooms had mosaic floors. In the middle room on the north side there is a mosaic with a medallion of Dionysos in the centre and animals, plants and human heads in separate frames round it, while at the top and bottom there is a band with two dogs (in the lower band they are chasing goats). The largest mosaic, in the north-west room, has numerous Dionysiac medallions (containing heads of Pan, sileni, satyrs and maenads) with supplementary subjects, such as birds and fishes, in the corners. The mosaic in the south-east room has heads in the corners and there was a head of Medusa in the centre.

Near here, to right and left of the road, the remains of a Roman amphitheatre and a Roman basilica have been found, while ruined Roman villas have been found in other places around Knossos. Continue along the main road and very soon you pass, on the right, the turning to the **Villa Ariadne.** This is the house which Evans built and used as his headquarters for the excavations at Knossos. In a separate building in the grounds of the villa is the **Stratigraphical Museum,** open to specialists only. It contains some whole vases, but most of the contents are sherds from the Knossos excavations. About 2,000 boxes of sherds from Evans' excavations were classified by J. Pendlebury, one of Evans' colleagues, who published the results of his work in his *Guide to the Stratigraphical Museum at Knossos,* 1933.

After the turning to the Villa Ariadne the road passes the **Little Palace** and the **Unexplored Mansion** (on the right), two very important Minoan buildings which will be described in the last chapter, and then you come immediately to the archaeological site of the palace of Knossos.

TOUR OF THE PALACE

The Main Features

As you approach the palace of Knossos you may find yourself wondering why the site was settled from such early times, from the first phase of the Neolithic in the 7th millennium B.C. The fact is that the hill of Kephala on which Neolithic man settled was in an exceptionally advantageous position, situated as it was in the fertile valley of the Kairatos river and only a short distance from the sea. The same site was used for the Prepalatial settlement at Knossos. Later it developed still more on account of its central position and it was here, in about 1900 B.C., that the largest and most important palace in Crete was built (Protopalatial period or MM IB to MM II according to Evans' chronological system). In 1700 the palace was utterly destroyed and rebuilt all over again (Neopalatial period or MM III to LM IIIA1 according to Evans' system) to be finally destroyed ca. 1375, by which time it had most probably been in the hands of overlords from Mycenaean Greece since 1450 (LM II according to Evans' system). Some scholars maintain that it was destroyed even later, perhaps as late as 1200 (end of LM IIIB according to Evans' system). To prepare the site for the construction of the palace, the top of the hill was levelled and stepped terraces and courts were made. Earth dumped from the modern excavations of the palace on the west slope of the hill has created the present deceptive impression that the palace did not stand on a hilltop.

Some elements have survived from all periods of the palace's history, but the palace visible today is actually the second palace of Knossos, the one built after the disaster of 1700 right on top of the ruins of the old palace. It also incorporates the additions and changes which were made after the earthquake of 1600. It is believed that its general plan did not differ much from that of its predecessor. Despite probable eastern influence, and *pace* Evans' theory that the palace was formed by joining together a number of separate square building units with rounded corners (Evans' *insulae*), the fact is that the overall plan of the palace appears to be an integrated complex of purpose-built rooms. It is roughly square in plan, with sides of about 150 metres, and it covers an area of 20,000 sq.m. It was almost twice as big as the palaces of Phaistos and Malia and three times larger than the palace at Zakros. Its dominant feature is the Central Court, nucleus of the whole complex and the heart of everyday life in the palace,

19. The Royal Road linked the palace of Knossos with the Little Palace.

20. Aerial view of the palace of Knossos from the west. In the foreground is the ▶ West Court, which is traversed by raised Processional Ways. Behind it is the West Wing, with part of its upper floor restored, and beyond that is the Central Court with the East Wing in the background.

and there was a second court on the west, facing you as you approach the site. There were several entrances on different sides, used for different purposes, and it seems that the rooms were arranged so that the cult places were situated in the West Wing and the residential quarters in the East Wing. It was obviously a multi-storeyed building.

The building materials used were stone, wood and clay. **Gypsum,** which was available in abundance from the neighbouring quarry on Gypsades hill, was used for wall-blocks, piers, steps, floor paving and the bases of columns and door jambs, while large thin slabs were used as a luxury facing on interior walls. **Limestone** was the commonest material for the walls (of ashlar masonry or rubble) as well as for paving stones, piers and pier bases, column bases, door and window frames, etc. **Schist** was used for floor paving. **Wood,** a basic material in the construction of the palace, was commonly used for columns, flooring in the upper storeys, roofing, stairs, door and window frames and the doors themselves. It was also used for another purpose: large vertical and horizontal beams were incorporated in the walls to hold them together and at the same time to give them a degree of flexibility, the better to withstand the frequent earthquakes. Finally, **clay** was used as a binding agent between the stones of the walls. Probably some parts of the upper storeys were built of clay bricks and the flat roofs covered with a layer of clay. The water pipes were also made of clay. The Minoans were also familiar with **lime plaster,** which was used to seal the exterior joints of ashlar facades (the courses were bonded together with clay). However, its main use was as a second coating, after clay, on rubble walls when a facing of gypsum slabs was not applied. So the interior walls were covered with a layer of clay followed by a coating of plaster, on which the wall-paintings with their wonderful Minoan themes were executed. Lime plaster was also used, either by itself or with the addition of potsherds or pebbles, for laying floors, usually out of doors, and frequently on the roofs, where it was placed as a final layer on top of the bedding of clay.

As is immediately apparent, the palace of Knossos has been restored in certain places by its excavator. These restorations have provoked sharp criticism, but in a good many cases they were necessary. Evans was obliged to support whatever he uncovered before proceeding to greater depth, because the wall beams had decayed and the walls had consequently disintegrated into heaps of stones. True, he went further, completing on a grand scale the sections he did restore. Nonetheless, if one looks carefully it is possible to distinguish between the authentic and the reconstructed, and such mistakes as have been made are negligible in relation to the immensity of the task. Furthermore, it must be admitted that the restorations in the palace of Knossos give one a better understanding of the function of the rooms and a stronger "feel" of the period, and that after seeing Knossos one is better able to visualise the other Minoan palaces which have been much less restored. Nowadays the prevailing tendency is simply to consolidate the monuments and protect them.

West Court – West Facade

A reconstructed ramp with low steps at intervals leads up towards the **West Court.** Behind us the traces of the original Minoan ramp are discernible, and in front of us is the enclosure which served as a retaining wall for the whole of the west side of the Court. At the point where the ramp meets the enclosure wall are the ruins of a room which Evans believed to have been the outer guardroom of the palace. On entering the West Court you will see a bronze bust of Arthur Evans, the excavator of Knossos. The bust was put up in 1935 and Evans himself was present at its unveiling. From this spot there is a wonderful view of the whole of the paved court with the facade of the palace in the background. The West Court was the ceremonial entrance to the palace and we should imagine it full of people moving to and fro, particularly on days of festivals and religious ceremonies. Formal processions followed the "Processional Ways", as the raised causeways traversing the West Court are called. Typical features of Minoan architecture, one of them leads straight across to the palace and the other runs diagonally to the left (north-east) towards the Theatral Area. Take the second (diagonal) Processional Way, which brings you to the three circular Walled Pits which the workmen in the excavation called *kouloures*. The Pits belong to the period of the first palace and were most probably sacred depositories, that is receptacles for the refuse from the palace shrines (used ritual vessels and remains of offerings). At the bottom of two of the kouloures one can see the remains of houses which were built in the final phase of the Prepalatial period, before the palace existed, and were subsequently buried beneath the paving of the Court. A staircase, walls and floor, all covered with red plaster, have survived from the house at the bottom of the middle kouloura. Numerous sherds of Kamares ware (that is fragments of vases of the MM II period, including egg-shell ware) were found in the kouloures, indicating that these depositories were in use during the Protopalatial period. When the second palace was built the kouloures fell into disuse and were covered over.

Cross the Court by the other Processional Way, which passes behind the bust of Evans and leads straight to the palace. The original flagstones of the Processional Way and the paved Court are easily distinguishable from the modern replacements. Right in front of the facade of the palace this causeway joins another Processional Way coming from the north. It is worth stopping here for a moment to look at the **West Facade:** huge upright gypsum slabs, the orthostates, stand on a projecting plinth of poros limestone. This levelling course, a common feature of Minoan architecture, is quite wide here and was perhaps used as a bench for people to sit on. Above the orthostates the wall has been reconstructed with double windows, though it is doubtful whether it was actually of ashlar masonry. Traces of the fire which destroyed the palace are clearly visible on the gypsum orthostates. In front of the West Facade there is a row of larger slabs in the paving which probably mark the line of the facade of the earlier palace. It can be seen that the East-West Causeway continues as far as the wall of the present facade, therefore it seems that this was the position of the West Entrance of the old palace, which led directly from the West Court into the Central Court. When the palace was rebuilt the entrance was moved to the south-west (on the right) and the facade was pushed back, leaving an area which was probably held sacred, for there is an altar base on this very spot. A recess in the wall just behind the altar indicates that there was a window higher up. If you go closer to the wall you can see how the bottom part of the West Facade was constructed: gypsum orthostates stood on both sides of the wall — inside and outside — and were held together by wooden cross-beams, as shown by the mortises on the gypsum slabs, while the space between them was filled with rubble. The upper part of the wall above the orthostates may also have been of rubble, coated with plaster. The West Magazines behind the facade on the ground floor are still visible, while above them there was a large room with a window overlooking the altar.

Before leaving the West Court turn left, following the raised walk northwards, in order to pay closer attention to the West Facade, which Evans maintained was three storeys high. At intervals along the wall there are projecting corners, a characteristic feature of Minoan architecture. Apart from their aesthetic effect, these projections enable us to gauge the position and form of the rooms in the upper storey, and wherever there is another smaller recess in the centre of each presumed room we may conclude that a window existed. So it is conjectured that there were three large rooms along the West Facade above the ground-floor Magazines. The first, behind the altar, has already been mentioned. The second has been partially restored with its window. Proceeding northwards along the raised walk you come to a second stone altar base on the left, while on the right a third large projection from the wall indicates the existence of a third large room, partially restored but with the window in the wrong place; it should have been in the shallow recess opposite the second altar. Go a little further north and you will see on the ground in front of you a large fragment of a gigantic pair of gypsum "horns of consecration", a sacred Minoan symbol. Beyond it you can see the Theatral Area, which is described later; on the right, in the north-west corner of the palace, there may have been a North-West Entrance. Return to the first altar base in order to enter the palace through the ceremonial entrance, the West Porch. (From now on see the Plan of the Palace of Knossos.)

21. Part of the West Facade of the palace, showing the projecting corners. The wall is faced with huge gypsum orthostates standing on a projecting plinth of poros limestone. In the foreground is the rectangular altar base.

22. Two of the "kouloures" in the West Court, with the West Facade of the palace behind.

PLAN OF THE PALACE OF KNOSSOS (after A. Evans)

A - C	I - XVIII West Magazines
1	Kouloures
2-2′	Altars
3	West Porch
4-4′-11	Corridor of the Procession
5	South-West Porch
6	Stepped Portico
7	South Terrace
8-8′	South Propylaeum
9	South Corridor
10	South Porch
11	Priest King Relief
12	Site of the Greek Temple
13	Bath-Tub with Linear B Tablets
14	Long Corridor of the West Magazines
15	Deposit of Hieroglyphic Tablets
16	Corridor of the Stone Basin
17	Anteroom of the Throne Room
18	Throne Room
19	Inner Sanctuary
20	Stepped Porch
21	Tripartite Shrine
22	Lobby of the Stone Seat
23	Temple Repositories
24	Pillar Crypts
25	Grand Staircase
26	Hall of the Double Axes (King's Hall)
27	Queen's Hall
28	Queen's Dressing Room
29	Court of the Distaffs
30	Service Staircase
31	South-East Bathroom
32	Shrine of the Double Axes
33	South-East Lustral Basin
34	Lobby of the Wooden Posts
35	East Portico
36	Lapidary's Workshop
37	School Room
38	Court of the Stone Spout
39	Magazines of the Giant Pithoi
40	East Bastion
41	Corridor of the Draughtboard
42	North-East Hall
43	North-East Magazines
44	Room of the Stone Drainhead
45	Magazine of the Medallion Pithoi
46	Corridor of the Bays
47	Early Keep
48	North Entrance Passage
49	North Pillar Hall
50	North Gate
51	North Lustral Basin and Initiatory Area
52	North-West Portico
53	Theatral Area
54	Royal Road
55	North-West Entrance?

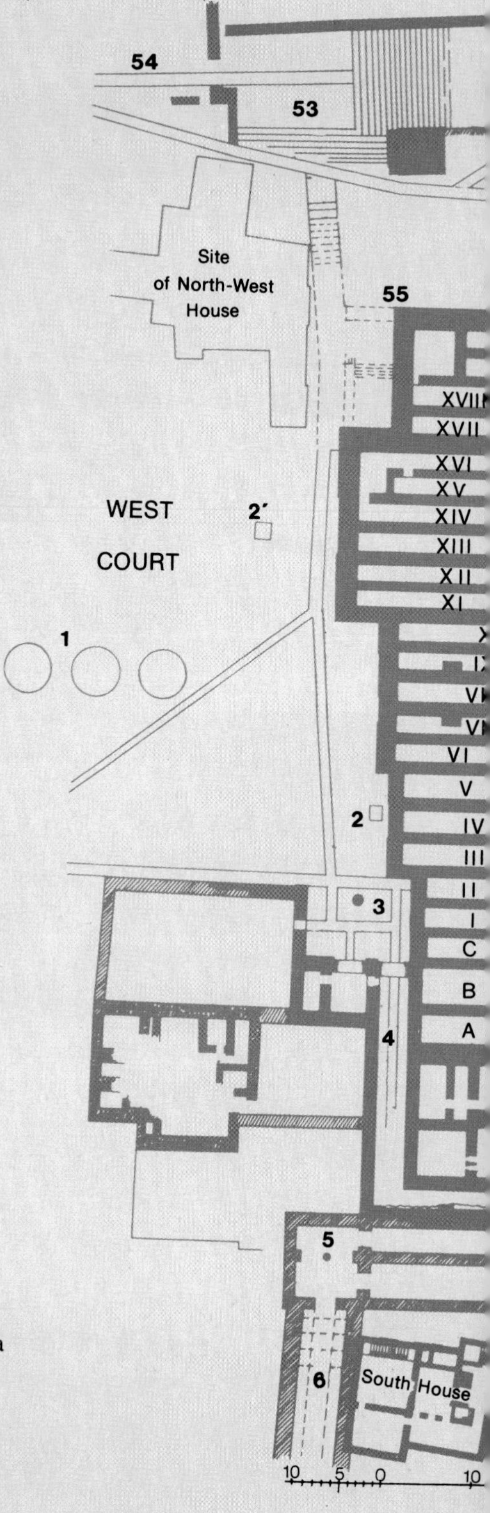

WEST COURT

Site of North-West House

South House

10 5 0 10

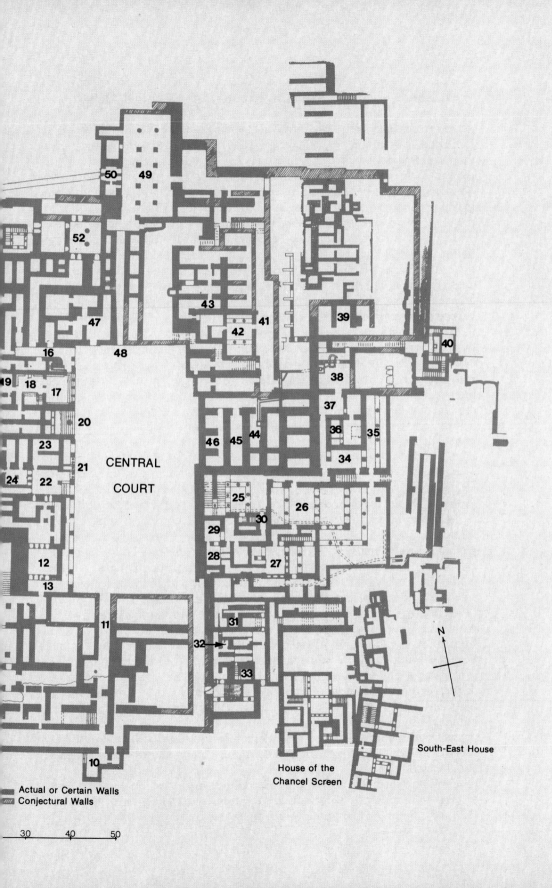

50 49

52

43

47

41
42

48

39

40

16

38

19 18
17

37

20

36 35

23

46 45 44

34

21

CENTRAL

24 22

COURT

25

26

30

29

28

27

12

13

11

31

32→

N

33

South-East House

10

House of the
Chancel Screen

■ Actual or Certain Walls
▧ Conjectural Walls

30   40   50

West Porch – Corridor of the Procession – Central Court

Go in through the **West Porch,** an open-fronted covered lobby which protected the entrance. On its east wall there was a wall-painting of a theme connected with the bull-games. A wooden column, part of the gypsum base of which is preserved, supported the roof. There are two doorways in front of you. The one on the right leads into a room with a red plaster floor and perhaps a place for a throne, with a smaller room off it to the west. We do not know if these were merely guardrooms controlling the entrance or if they served some ceremonial purpose. The other doorway, on the left, still has pivot-holes on either side for the double doors which once closed the official entrance to the palace, and a third hole in the centre of the door-sill for the vertical locking bolt. Stretching away in front of you is a long passageway known as the **Corridor of the Procession,** so named after the wall-painting which covered the walls of the corridor along its entire length and depicted a procession of almost life-size men and women bearing gifts and sacred vessels or musical instruments, with a central figure representing a goddess or priestess. What survives of the wall-painting is now in the Herakleion Museum. One can imagine the impression this fresco made on the visitor to the palace as he walked along the corridor amidst painted figures of gift-bearers, musicians and perhaps priests. He would feel as if he belonged to their company and, without doubt, there would have been days when such formal processions would have wended their way along the raised walks of the West Court and then along the Corridor of the Procession. It is very significant that this corridor, after turning two right-angled corners to the left, led either to the South Propylaeum and from there to the state apartments on the first floor, or else to the Central Court of the palace. The floor of the corridor is superb, with a raised walk of gypsum slabs in the centre and, to right and left, crazy paving of green schist with red plaster in the interstices. Follow the corridor along its extant section, as far as the small modern staircase, beyond which the Corridor of the Procession turned left and continued along the south side of the palace, above the rooms still visible at the lower ground level. Facing you now are the restored ruins of the **South House,** which will be described in the chapter on the dependencies of the palace. Just in front of it are the ruins of another entrance to the palace, the famous **Stepped Portico** which was constructed, according to Evans, during the Protopalatial period. Until the earthquake of 1600 B.C., when it was abandoned (end of the first Neopalatial phase), it was used by travellers from the interior of Crete who, after resting at the **Caravanserai,** a Minoan building discovered to the south of the palace, crossed the famous Minoan viaduct and mounted the Stepped Portico to the **South-West Porch** (the ruins visible on your right), from where they followed the **South Terrace** parallel with the Corridor of the Procession and just south of it.

From the surviving part of the Corridor of the Procession you now have to take an unorthodox short cut through the restored section of the room with the column and so to the **South Propylaeum,** the west side of which

23. The West Porch was the ceremonial entrance to the palace. In the foreground is the stone base of its single wooden column, and the beginning of the Corridor of the Procession can be seen in the background at left.

has been restored. Processions would have turned through this portico in order to proceed to the upper floor. Carry on further eastwards, however, towards the large horns. Made of poros limestone and restored, they denote the sanctity of the area, for the "horns of consecration" are a Minoan religious symbol perhaps derived from the horns of the sacred bull. Looking south from this position you can see below you the lower ground level apartments that lay under the Corridor of the Procession. Beyond them is the South Terrace and beyond that the **South Corridor,** which terminated above the **South Porch** located in a bastion-like projection of the palace. This entrance was probably of secondary importance and used mainly after the earthquake which destroyed the Stepped Portico. (Underneath the entrance Evans found an immense subterranean vaulted chamber hewn out

24. Reconstruction drawing of the Stepped Portico. Visitors from the interior of Crete would have crossed over the famous Minoan viaduct and walked up the Stepped Portico to enter the palace by the South-West Porch. (Drawn by Thomas Fanourakis)

of the soft rock. It had an external spiral staircase and was perhaps a granary of the Prepalatial period.) From the same spot, near the horns, you can see Gypsades hill, where there are Minoan gypsum quarries, cemeteries and houses, and, in the background, the summit of Mt. Juktas, where an important Minoan Peak Sanctuary was found. Cretan myths place the tomb of Zeus on Mt. Juktas and the mountain does actually look like the silhouette of a gigantic supine head when seen from a certain position further west.

Keep walking eastwards beyond the pair of horns and turn left into the restored sector with the column and the wall-painting of the **Prince of the Lilies.** This was the final stretch of the Corridor of the Procession, as is evident from the identical paving of the floor. It was lit by a colonnaded light-well and on the opposite wall was the famous relief fresco of the Prince of the Lilies. What you see here is a copy of the original, which is on display in the Herakleion Museum. It depicts a regal figure, perhaps the priest-king, wearing a crown of lilies with peacock plumes and with his left hand apparently leading something or someone towards the Central Court. He may have been at the head of the figures in the wall-painting of the procession, leading a sphinx (as shown in a comparable relief on a Mycenaean ivory pyxis) or a griffin (according to Evans). Immediately beyond this fresco the visitor coming from the West Court along the Corridor of the Procession entered the Central Court, and at this point it is possible to envisage the palace as an entity.

The **Central Court** is the nucleus of the palace. Orientated on a north-south axis, its dimensions are approximately 50 × 25 m. or 165 × 82.50 Minoan feet (1 Minoan foot = 0.3036 m.). The palaces of Anatolia also have a central Court; however, the Minoan palace differs because it is not confined by an outer enclosure wall (the one bounding the West Court is there because it acts as a retaining wall) but developed from the inside outwards: it was organised around the Central Court and spread unevenly towards the four points of the compass, with the West and East Wings as the main units. The Central Court provided the palace apartments with light and air, and every movement to and from the various sectors of the palace started and finished there. The existence of shrines facing on to the Central Court indicates that religious ceremonies were held there as well as in the West Court. Perhaps the bull-games, the ritual sport beloved of the Minoans, also took place in the Central Court (Professor J.W. Graham's opinion), though another school of thought holds that the arena was located outside the East Wing of the palace beside the bed of the Kairatos river (Evans' opinion). We should imagine the Court paved, as it still is in its north-west part. On the left rose the two or three storeys of the West Wing, with its shrines and storerooms on the ground floor and other shrines and reception halls above. Looking along this facade from south to north you can see, first, a series of restored piers with indications of columns on top of them, which supported a verandah overlooking the Central Court; then the sector with the Pillar Crypts and the Tripartite Shrine — now protected by a roof — and further on, beyond a wide

25. *The South Propylaeum and "horns of consecration" seen from the South Porch (bottom right), with the South Corridor and South Terrace in the foreground.*

staircase, the restored antechamber of the Throne Room. On the right the East Wing towered above the Court to a height of two or three storeys. Here were the Domestic Quarters with the royal storerooms and workshops. Below the level of the Court there were a further two storeys, since a deep cutting into the east slope of the hill created successive terraces with a wonderful view of the river Kairatos. The most impressive of the staircases communicating between the four or five storeys was the Grand Staircase — visible under the modern roof near the middle of the east facade of the Court — while further north, where you can see a concrete floor with railings, one should probably imagine the East Hall, a large reception hall with a wide columned staircase leading up from the Central Court. Facing you at the far end is the restored verandah above the West

Bastion of the North Entrance Passage, which led to the North Entrance of the palace. For in addition to the probable entrance at the north-west corner of the palace, the ceremonial West Porch, the South-West Porch (approached by the Stepped Portico) and the South Porch, there was a North Entrance where the harbour road ended, and yet another entrance in the East Wing which gave access, through a bastion, from the Kairatos river. We should imagine the palace with flat roofs at different heights (with "horns of consecration" on the roofs of the shrines), with wooden columns tapering towards the base and with a system of light-wells which were, after the Courts, the principal means of illuminating and ventilating the rooms in each Wing.

South Propylaeum – West Magazines – Piano Nobile

From the end of the Corridor of the Procession return to the area in front of the **South Propylaeum.** This most impressive monument consisted of two porches with two columns each, guarding the central gate on its north and south sides. The south side of the Propylaeum was closed by three doors; the bases of the jambs and part of the threshold of the easternmost door have survived. Also preserved are the bases of two columns (slightly elliptical on a square plinth) and the lower parts of the walls, which show that the South Propylaeum was initially wider: on the reconstructed west wall you can see concrete imitations of the original timber tie-beams reinforcing the rubble wall and copies of frescoes portraying figures advancing to meet those depicted in the Corridor of the Procession or carrying sacred vessels for the ceremonies in the West Court. The young Minoan at bottom right is called the "Cup-Bearer" after the large conical rhyton he is holding (a rhyton being a ritual vessel for libations). Go up the two steps of the main doorway into the north section of the South Propylaeum and you will see a number of storage jars (pithoi), which were placed here after the destruction of the palace, in the so-called "Reoccupation Period" (LM IIIB). Both the staircase in front of you and the floor of the upper storey, to which it leads, were reconstructed in concrete by Evans, mainly to protect the rooms below but also to restore the large halls which once existed on the first floor — the *Piano Nobile* as Evans named it, using the architectural terminology of the Italian Renaissance. The restoration was made on the basis of architectural observations on the ground floor and finds, such as column bases and fragments of wall-paintings, which had fallen from the first floor. The imposing staircase had colonnaded verandahs to right and left. From the top landing you look down on to a square room to the right of the staircase, with an extensively restored paved floor and plumbing installations beneath. To the south a clay bathtub was found containing Linear B tablets. In the course of the excavation Evans found and dismantled a Greek temple dedicated to the goddess Rhea (or, according to Professor L.R. Palmer, a Mycenaean *megaron),* which stood on top of this room. From the landing go through one of the two doors facing you, into a lobby (see the plan of the Piano

Nobile) and from there into a large hall, on the floor of which there are three column bases and three pier bases (most of them are the original ones which Evans found fallen into the ground floor and replaced here). Evans, inspired by scenes in wall-paintings, called the area the **Tricolumnar Shrine.** Off the south-east corner of the Shrine there is a square room which is believed to have been its **Treasury** because a large number of precious ritual vessels had fallen from there into the ground floor. Perhaps these vessels were conveyed by the Minoans along the Corridor of the Procession to the West Court, where the stone altars were.

From the west side of the Tricolumnar Shrine the famous **West Magazines** of the ground floor are visible below. These were eighteen long, narrow storerooms — there were originally three more further south — which opened on to a long corridor running north-south. Nowadays this Long Corridor has been fenced off from the IIIrd to the XIIth magazine, so it is easier to see them from the upper floor. Evans roofed storerooms VIII to XII with concrete. The walls of the magazines facing the corridor are faced with gypsum orthostates (vertical slabs), blackened by the fire which destroyed the palace and was particularly fierce here because of the stores of oil. In each magazine, along the walls, there were rows of enormous pithoi full of oil or wine, and in the centre, under the floor, a row of stone cists — some lined with lead — which Evans' workmen called *kaselles*. There were also kaselles under the floor of the Long Corridor and even beneath the thresholds of some magazines (VII, VIII, IX). There were ninety-eight sunken cists in all, and they were used for the safe keeping of precious objects or, if coated with plaster inside, for liquids. The storerooms were probably lit only by oil lamps. The Long Corridor had a wooden ceiling and was blocked at its southern end (before magazine IV) by a transverse wall which still has the remains of door-posts attached. This door provided additional security for the magazines. It has been estimated that the storerooms could hold more than four hundred pithoi with a total capacity of 78,000 litres. There were several building phases in the magazines, as is indicated by the different kinds of flooring, the addition of smaller *kaselles* inside earlier ones and the narrowing of some doorways by a wall built at a later date. Note the pyramidal stone bases in front of certain magazines: these were stands for double axes, a religious symbol of the Minoans. There are also double axes incised on the walls of the magazines along with other symbols: star, branch and cross, the last of these sometimes inscribed in a square. All this, coupled with the fact that the magazines communicated directly with the sacred Pillar Crypts on the ground floor (which are described later), indicates that the West Magazines had some connection with the shrines of the West Wing.

Coming out by the north door of the Tricolumnar Shrine, you will see on the right a wide staircase descending to the Central Court. Do not go

26. The South Propylaeum. The west side of this great portico has been restored and is adorned with a copy of the Cup-Bearer Fresco. In the background is the restored monumental stairway leading to the Piano Nobile (the upper floor).

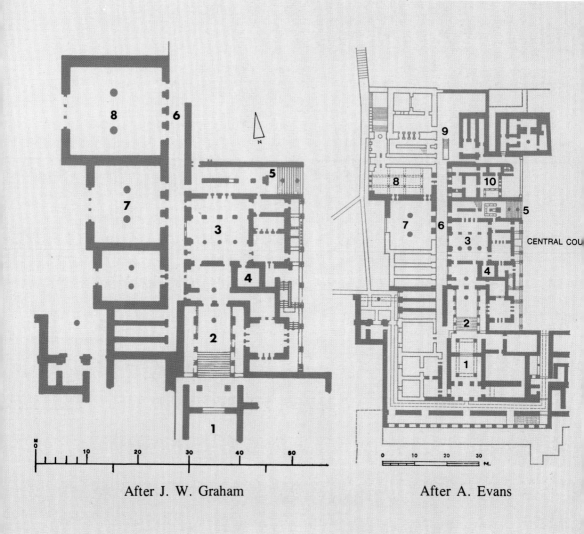

After J. W. Graham   After A. Evans

KNOSSOS: PIANO NOBILE (First Floor)

1 South Propylaeum
2 Staircase up from South Propylaeum
3 Tricolumnar Shrine
4 Treasury of the Shrine
5 Staircase down to the Central Court
6 Upper Long Corridor
7 Great Hall
8 Sanctuary Hall
9 Stairs down to the West Magazines
10 Restored room with replicas of frescoes

down it but turn left into the Upper Long Corridor, which is directly above the Long Corridor of the Magazines. In all probability it was unroofed to let light into the rooms on either side. To the west of the corridor were the large reception halls of the palace. Evans partially restored two rooms: the one with two columns was named the **Great Hall** and the more northerly one with six columns he called the **Sanctuary Hall.** The existence of a sanctuary here was deduced from the wall-paintings of religious subjects found on the ground floor, where they had fallen. The arrangement of the ground-floor rooms leads to the conclusion that there were three large first-floor rooms right on top of the West Magazines. The south-west one was above magazines III to V. The middle one (coinciding with Evans' Great Hall) was on top of magazines VI to X: massive piers were built in magazines VII and IX to support the two first-floor columns which were necessary for the roofing of the Great Hall. Finally, the north-west room, larger than the others, was situated in the place where Evans restored the Sanctuary Hall, but in all probability its size and shape were different. Enter the Sanctuary Hall and go over to the west side. From the window, which has been restored in the wrong place, you have an unimpeded view over the West Court. From the northernmost edge of the restored floor of the Sanctuary Hall it is apparent that the room must have extended further to the north, as far as the north wall of magazine XVI, which is thicker for the very reason that it was designed to support the weight of the upper wall. Consequently the north-west room was above magazines XI to XVI and perhaps had two columns instead of six (J.W. Graham's conjecture). This magnificent room, like the adjacent one, may have been a reception hall. North of it there seems to have been a North-West Entrance to the palace: a large external staircase presumably led directly to the first-floor reception halls and to another room east of the staircase, above magazines XVII and XVIII and the two small adjacent rooms. In the background you can see the Theatral Area.

Return now to the Upper Long Corridor and go down the modern flight of steps at the north end of its east wall. This joins a staircase which in Minoan times led from the first floor to the northern part of the Long Corridor of the Magazines, coming out opposite magazine XIV, so it is possible to see some of the storerooms at close quarters. Beyond the railings the Long Corridor is visible with its pithoi and the pyramidal double-axe stands. Outside the railings there is an incised branch symbol on the orthostate of magazine XIII. Magazines XIV, XV and XVI were blocked off at some time, but they can be visited through magazine XVII. The long, narrow space behind the stairs was used as an archive room, for tablets inscribed in hieroglyphic script were found here. Keeping accounts of the produce stored in the magazines required a bureaucratic system, which is attested both by these earlier hieroglyphic archives and by the numerous Linear B tablets found in the area of the West Magazines in the first few days of the excavation.

Go back up the staircase and turn left into a restored room in which replicas of Minoan wall-paintings are exhibited. Here we have an oppor-

27. *A restored light-well on the first floor of the West Wing. On the walls of the room which looks on to the light-well are copies of frescoes which were found in the palace and the House of the Frescoes.*

28. *One of the magazines, i.e. store-rooms, on the ground floor of the West Wing. Enormous pithoi stand in rows along the walls, and in the middle of the room, under the floor, there is a row of stone cists known as "kaselles".*

27

tunity of seeing how bull-leaping was done and what the "Tripartite Shrine" looked like. In the south part of the room the restored upper portion of a light-well gives us an idea of how this widely-used system of admitting light and air to the internal rooms actually worked. If you lean over the low parapet of the light-well you can see below you the Lustral Basin of the Throne Room complex, which is the next part of the palace to be visited. To reach it, go out on to the restored open terrace and down the spiral staircase on its north side. The staircase is set in the angle of a rounded corner which in Evans' opinion belonged to the first phase of the palace: he maintained that it was one of the corners of the *insula* which existed there previously.

Throne Room – Tripartite Shrine – Pillar Crypts

If you turn left at the bottom of the staircase you come out into the corridor which has been named the **Corridor of the Stone Basin,** because it was here that the porphyry basin now in the anteroom to the Throne Room was found; and if you follow this corridor to its end you come back to the north end of the Long Corridor of the Magazines. So turn right at the foot of the stairs, go down three steps and into the **Anteroom of the Throne Room.** Stone benches of gypsum, blackened by the fire which destroyed the palace, are set against the north and south walls and on the east there are four doors opening on to the Central Court. A wooden replica of the throne has been placed on the spot where Evans found a quantity of charred wood. The floor is typically Minoan, consisting of gypsum flagstones around a central square of black ironstone crazy paving with red plaster in the interstices. In the middle of the room stands the porphyry basin which Evans believed contained water for the purification of those about to enter the Throne Room.

Through the double portal with modern wooden railings you can look into the **Throne Room.** Stone benches run round three of its walls, with a space in the centre of the north wall to accommodate the famous Throne of Minos. This was one of Evans' first finds: it was discovered on this very spot and is probably the oldest known throne in Europe. In recent times it has been used as the model for the chair of the President of the International Court at the Hague. The throne is made of gypsum in imitation of a wooden original, with traces of red and white plaster still visible on it. To right and left of the throne are copies of the famous wall-painting with the griffins, those mythical creatures with lion's body and eagle's head. In the south part of the room, separated by a bench and a balustrade with wooden columns (charred traces of the columns were found) is a rectangular space with a sunken floor laid with gypsum flags. A flight of six steps leads down

29. The Anteroom of the Throne Room. The porphyry basin in the middle was placed here by Evans. Against the north wall is a replica of a wooden throne with stone benches on either side.

into it. The walls all around are faced with a dado of gypsum slabs, with red plaster above. Areas with this architectural form have been named **Lustral Basins**; it is believed that they were used for some type of ritual to cleanse body and soul, and similar ones have been found in the north-west and south-east sectors of the palace. On the floor of the Throne Room Evans found some stone libation vessels (squat alabastra) and so believed that the destruction of the palace interrupted a ceremony which was taking place at that very moment. Perhaps it was a ritual to appease the divinity and so avert the earthquake. Both the layout and the finds, as well as the fact that the Throne Room is located on the ground floor of the West Wing, clearly indicate that it had a religious function. The actual Throne Room, that is the audience chamber of the king, should perhaps be sought in the large East Hall of the East Wing. On the throne we now see before us we should imagine the king officiating in his capacity as High Priest at various ceremonies, while around him sat the rest of the priests, numbering as many as sixteen. It is very likely, however, that it was the queen-priestess who sat on the throne rather than the king, because the deity whom she represented is usually shown accompanied by griffins. This deity is the great Mother Goddess, the creative force of nature who appears in various guises, such as goddess of the mountains, mistress of animals, *kourotro-phos* (holding a child), chthonic deity and even goddess of war. However, the youthful god who is represented as her husband or son and dies each year with the vegetation, to be resurrected the following year, is also depicted as master of animals accompanied by a winged moufflon or a griffin. There is also the young goddess of vegetation, who survives in ancient Greek religion in the person of Persephone. This limited Minoan pantheon seems to have dwelt in three worlds— the heavens, the earth and the underworld — and from these stem also the various attributes of the mother goddess mentioned above. Ultimately the question of who sat on this throne is related to the problem of how strongly matriarchal tendencies persisted in the Minoan civilisation. It would appear that survivals from a matriarchal past lingered on in the religion and in the organisation of the priesthood, for not only is the dominant deity a goddess but frequently too the priests are portrayed wearing female attire.

A door in the west wall of the Throne Room led into the **Inner Sanctuary,** a dark chamber lit by an oil lamp and with a masonry pedestal (probably used as a stand for sacred symbols and ritual vessels) against the back wall opposite the door. Opening off it was another room in which there are two pithoi and a fine example of the cross-in-square symbol carved on stones; a similar one was found carved on the wall of the Lustral

◀ *30. The Throne Room. The famous gypsum throne was found* in situ, *flanked by stone benches. The paintings on the walls are copies of the original frescoes of griffins.*

31. The Throne Room seen from the Lustral Basin. (Courtesy of the National Geographic Magazine)

32. The Temple Repositories, where precious ritual vessels and works of art, including the snake goddesses, were found in rectangular cists sunk in the floor.

Basin, under the red plaster. The entire Throne Room complex is considered to be one of the latest parts of the palace, dating perhaps from the years of Mycenaean suzerainty (1450 – ca. 1375). Even though nothing resembling it has been found in the other Minoan palaces (precisely because in about 1450 they were destroyed and abandoned, while Knossos survived), nonetheless the details are Minoan, especially the Lustral Basin. That the entire complex was a later addition to the West Wing (where the shrines had always been) is indicated by the walls of the rooms to north and west of the suite, which have been cut; these rooms served as auxiliary offices used in preparing for the ceremonies presumed to have been held in the Throne Room.

One can glance into the room in the north-east corner through the opening (closed by a grille) which looks on to the Corridor of the Stone

33. Part of the west facade of the Central Court, showing the doors leading into the Throne Room and the imposing stairway leading up to the first floor.

Basin. Inside this room you can see a low block of dressed stone which Evans named the "Lady's Seat". In an adjacent room there is a masonry pedestal and a tall stone cylinder with two cavities (perhaps used for grinding wheat in the preparation of food for religious rites). In the last (south-west) room, which Evans originally called the **Kitchen,** the same type of seat was found in front of a low table with cavities and, at the back, a low stepped plaster dais with a circular depression in the middle. Finally, another door in the Throne Room, located in the south wall behind the Lustral Basin, gives access to a long, narrow chamber with three large rectangular cists in which precious objects were stored. All these rooms around the Throne Room, submerged in the half-light, have a somewhat mysterious atmosphere. When you are in them you really feel that you are in the depths of the palace. You feel the palace coming to life around you,

and you should not be too surprised if you are aware of a momentary fear that someone may come and catch you trespassing....

Leave the Anteroom of the Throne Room by the multiple doors into the Central Court, where you will see part of the drainage system which traversed the Court to carry away the rain-water. Then turn right (southwards) to visit the remaining rooms of the West Wing. First you pass a magnificent staircase, mainly restored, which leads up to the Piano Nobile. The first four steps are preserved, and so are parts of the bases of two columns which stood in the centre of the stairway to support the roof of a porch opening on to the Central Court. The staircase was built in the LM I period at the earliest, because it passes over some large rectangular cists of the MM III period (one of which can be seen beneath the gap on the left at the sixth step). At the landing there is a passage straight ahead on the left side, leading to the first-floor apartments (the Tricolumnar Shrine, with the reception halls further west), while on the right the staircase narrows and continues up to a second floor or to the flat roof. The evidence for the continuation of the staircase includes some small fragments of the original steps and traces left by the steps on the landing block under the little column.

Continuing southwards, just beyond the staircase you come to a stylobate with faint traces of two round column bases on it. Here, in the middle of the west facade of the Central Court, Evans located the **Tripartite Shrine,** on the evidence of the wall-painting of that name. It consisted of three sections, the central section being elevated, with a single column, and the lateral ones lower down, with a pair of columns each. Essentially it was merely a facade, surmounted by pairs of horns. Only behind the central section does there appear to have been a small rectangular room, in which Linear B tablets were found. Behind the right-hand section — where the earlier paving of the Court and the earlier facade with gypsum orthostates have survived — the excavators found seal impressions in clay, depicting the Mistress of Animals. It is tempting to assume that the Tripartite Shrine sybolised the three worlds of the Minoan pantheon: the heavens in the elevated central section, the earth on the right, where the sealings were found, and the underworld in the left-hand section, behind which is the vestibule to the dark, sacred Pillar Crypts.

Go down the stairs into the antechamber of the Crypts, or the **Lobby of the Stone Seat** as it is called after the impressive bench on the north wall. The bench is blackened by fire and in the wall behind it one can see that horizontally-laid slabs of gypsum have been used as building material, which is most unusual. The floor is of the same kind as in the Throne Room and its anteroom. Visit first the two rooms to the north: the **Room of the Tall Pithos** and the room containing the **Temple Repositories,** two large

◄ *34. Reconstruction drawing of the west facade of the Central Court. To the right of the imposing staircase is the Throne Room complex; to the left, the Tripartite Shrine. (Drawn by Thomas Fanourakis)*

rectangular cists sunk into the floor, in which were found precious ritual vessels and works of art, including the famous snake goddesses. They belong to the MM IIIB period and were later covered over and replaced by other, smaller cists, of which the middle one can still be seen (LM I period).

Return to the Lobby and go over to the two doors in the west wall, now closed by a grille. These led into the **Pillar Crypts.** The East Crypt had a square pillar in the centre flanked by two stone basins set into the floor. Two rooms opened off it to the north: the Vat Room and the room with the low stone ledge. These may have been the sacristies of the crypts. Off it to the west is a second crypt, the West Crypt, with a square pillar in the centre, a square sunken floor around it and a high bench along the east wall. Pillar crypts were household shrines found not only in the palaces but also in private houses of the Minoan era. Dark chambers, with the pillar like an abstract representation of the deity, they were related to the cult of the chthonic powers which revitalise the earth. Incised on the pillars is the sacred symbol of the double axe, three times on the pillar in the East Crypt and twenty-nine times on the pillar in the West Crypt. Blood offerings or bloodless sacrifices were placed in the basins and the square trough round the pillar, and remains of sacrifices were found beneath the floor of the East Crypt. It is significant that the crypts communicated directly both with the Temple Repositories and with the West Magazines. The third door in the west wall of the Lobby is open. Go through it into a corridor, past the back door of the West Crypt on the right and on to the end of the corridor, where the south part of the Long Corridor of the Magazines can be seen through a grille. From there you have to retrace your steps to the Central Court. It is now possible to envisage the **Central Shrine** of the West Wing as a whole. There was the facade — the Tripartite Shrine — facing the Central Court, behind that on the ground floor were the Lobby, the Crypts, the sacristies and the Temple Repositories, and on the upper floor the Tricolumnar Shrine with its Treasury.

Further south on the west facade of the Central Court you can see the restored verandah from which the Minoans watched what was happening in the Court. Still visible behind the pillars are the gypsum orthostates of the earlier west facade which was abandoned after the earthquake in 1600 B.C., when the facade was shifted further east.

Grand Staircase – Hall of the Double Axes – Queen's Hall

The next part of the palace to be visited is the East Wing, in the south part of which are the Domestic Quarters and in the north the Royal Workshops and Storerooms. A great vertical cutting into the east slope of the hill created a terrace big enough to accommodate the four (or five) storeys of the East Wing, two of which were below the level of the Court.

To visit these lower levels first, cross over to the east side of the Central Court and go down the **Grand Staircase.** Protected beneath a modern roof, the staircase is situated near the middle of the East Wing and is the crowning achievement of Minoan architecture. Almost five flights are preserved, the two lower ones exactly as they were found. Its gypsum steps, with their broad, shallow treads, make an easy descent. The staircase is lit by a large light-well to the east, surrounded on three sides by colonnades at different levels and on the south by a wall with double windows. The columns on the side nearest the staircase stood on a stepped parapet: the sockets into which their bases fitted are still visible and the columns have been restored. Minoan columns were generally wooden, as were their capitals, which is why they have not survived. However, they stood on stone bases which give evidence of their presence. Unlike ancient Greek columns, they tapered towards the base, and a number of explanations have been advanced for this: that it was for aesthetic reasons, or to ensure more free space between the columns, or for practical reasons such as protecting the base from the rain, etc. Certainly the downward taper of the Minoan column made it particularly suitable for the successive colonnades much beloved of the Minoan people. Walk down the staircase to the bottom; you are now two storeys below the level of the Central Court, in the area which Evans named the **Hall of the Colonnades.** Follow the corridor from west to east, ignoring the door on the right which leads into the Queen's Apartments, and proceed to the door facing you. The floor of the corridor is in an excellent state of preservation, with alternate wide and narrow slabs: even the marks made on it by the scraping of the wooden door are still visible, and so is the rectangular pivot-hole of the door. After a double window on the right there is a door which leads directly to the King's Quarters. From here onwards, surprise and astonishment await you at every step....

The entire complex of the Domestic Quarters seems to have extended over successive floors which communicated with each other via the Grand Staircase and three other stairways. All the rooms are at the same time private yet interconnected by corridors. It is amazing how long one can spend wandering in and out of these rooms, going up and down stairs and frequently, much to one's surprise, finding oneself back in the same room having come by a different route. Four light-wells (besides that of the Grand Staircase) and a "light area" (a kind of walled-in yard) admit light and air to the suite. Pier-and-door partitions permit the rooms to be opened up into suites or closed off from each other, thus ensuring coolness or warmth according to the prevailing weather conditions. The King's Hall is a double room. The west half, in which you are standing, is lit by a light-well with two columns in front. Incised on the ashlar masonry of the light-well are many examples of the double-axe symbol, which is why Evans called the King's Hall the **Hall of the Double Axes.** One of the two

35. The Grand Staircase in the East Wing is generally regarded as the crowning achievement of Minoan architecture. A stepped balustrade with columns separates the staircase from a large light-well, which is bounded on two sides by a series of superimposed colonnades and on its south side by a wall with double windows.

36. Reconstruction drawing of the Hall of the Double Axes, by Piet de Jong. The room was kept warm in winter with portable hearths.

columns of the light-well was found preserved, though badly charred, to a length of 2.60 metres. Evans noted that it was made from the trunk of a cypress tree and that it had a downward taper of 10 cm. On the north wall of the room, under the protective glass cover, there is a mass of calcified gypsum which had fallen down and covered the wooden throne that once stood on this spot. The eastern half of the room, now fenced off by railings, is of the *polythyron* type, i.e. with pier-and-door partitions: it has sets of four doors on two sides and a set of three on the south side. The east and south sides open on to a colonnade which faces an L-shaped light area. The stone bases of the jambs of the multiple doors have survived and so have the pivot-holes, which show that each doorway had double doors. When the doors were opened both leaves folded back into recesses in the jambs and the wall then became a row of piers. Thus the King's Hall could either be one large room with the multiple doors open or two separate rooms when the doors were closed. In the summer the warm air rose up the west light-well and cooler air was drawn in through the doors opening on to the colonnades, giving a type of air-conditioning. In the winter the doors

37. The restored Hall of the Double Axes as it is today, with a replica of the king's wooden throne set against the wall.

on to the colonnades were closed and portable hearths heated the double room. Gypsum slabs were used for the floor paving and as a facing for the walls up to a certain height, above which there was a continuous spiral painted on the wall plaster. Large figure-of-eight shields similar to those depicted in a wall-painting may have been hung above the gypsum dado on the wall behind the replica of the throne. The shields were made of oxhide and their shape was intended to ward off enemy blows.

Leave the Hall of the Double Axes through a door in the south wall, next to the light-well (note the remarkable plumbing system in the floor of the light-well). This takes you along a dog-leg corridor, the walls of which are faced with enormous gypsum slabs that have suffered the ravages of fire, and so into the **Queen's Hall.** Just next to the door there is another door (now closed) behind which is a private staircase leading to the upper storey. The walls of the Queen's Hall are adorned with copies of the Dolphin Fresco (north wall) and the Dancing Girl Fresco (in the embrasure of one of the windows). A later fresco of continuous spirals was painted over an earlier one with a design of rosettes. The uninterrupted use of this

38. Reconstruction drawing of the Queen's Hall, by Piet de Jong. The multiple windows look out on to two light-wells, one on the east side and one on the south.

room is attested by the successive layers of paving under the grille in the floor of the room. Two light-wells, one on the east and one on the south, illuminate the room through multiple windows in those two walls (on the east side there is a two-columned portico between the windows and the light-well). It is not certain whether there were wooden benches like those which have been constructed in concrete, but one would certainly have been able to sit on the wooden window-sill to admire the flowers which perhaps grew in the east light-well. Go out into this light-well, through the door in the south wall of its portico and left into the light area in front of the colonnades of the Hall of the Double Axes. (This gave the queen an alternative route for going to visit the king, in addition to the dog-leg corridor.) In the north wall of the light area there is a door on to a landing, from which one could turn left to an external staircase to the upper floor, or go straight ahead into a colonnade (the East Portico, which we shall see later when we visit the workshop sector), or turn right down the continuation of the staircase to the lower terraces.

Return to the Queen's Hall in order to visit her **Bathroom,** located to

39. The Queen's Hall as it is today, after restoration. Next to the entrance door is another door (now closed by a grille) leading to a staircase to the upper floor.

the west of the Hall, from which it is separated by a wall with a large window. It still has a parapet with a single column, which has been restored with fluting on the strength of examples from the Little Palace at Knossos. The clay bathtub placed here was found in pieces near the doorway and in the main room. To the left of the bathroom is the entrance to a dark corridor which leads to the Queen's **Dressing Room.** This is a rectangular room with a low rectangular platform in the south-west corner, perhaps for her toiletries. The room is lit by a window and door opening on to a light-well, which has been named the **Court of the Distaffs** from the symbol incised on its walls. It seems to have been yet another small private courtyard for the use of the queen. The ledge at the bottom of the north wall is sufficiently deep to have served as a bench. Off the Dressing Room to the east is a small rectangular room which is formed by partition walls of double upright gypsum slabs. This was the **Queen's Privy.** The grooves cut in the walls and floor indicate that there was a wooden seat above the large drain at the end. On the floor of the Dressing Room, in front of the privy, there is a slightly concave flagstone with a hole through which clean water was flushed into the drain. Continue northwards along a dimly-lit corridor and in the floor on the left you can see another section of the drains. (The layout of the drainage circuit is quite remarkable: it passes under the Grand Staircase and the King's and Queen's Halls and channels all the water from the water closet and light-wells eastwards into the river.) On the right you pass by a closed room in which clay sealings and remains of precious objects were found, and on turning left you come to the bottom of the Service Staircase which leads to the restored upper apartments of the queen. In the empty space on the left, under the stairs, the wonderful ivory figure of the bull-leaper was found together with other pieces from the complete tableau of the bull-games. Go through the door in front of you and you are back in the Hall of the Colonnades. The layout of the rooms in the Domestic Quarter is quite remarkable. For example, there were five different ways of getting to the Queen's Hall: from the Hall of the Colonnades you could go either though the door you have just come out of, or through the King's Hall and along the dog-leg corridor, or through the King's Hall and out through the colonnade and light area to the queen's light-well, and there were also two staircases from the upper floor: the Service Staircase and the Private Staircase behind the barred doorway in the Queen's Hall.

Upper Floor of the Domestic Quarter – Shrine of the Double Axes – South-East Lustral Basin

Go up the Grand Staircase into the Upper Hall of the Colonnades, which is decorated with a copy of the wall-painting of the figure-of-eight shields and is also called the **Hall of the Royal Guard.** There would certainly have been guards permanently posted on each landing of the Grand Staircase to check on the persons going in and out of the royal apartments, workshops and storerooms. Follow the Upper West-East Corridor, going eastwards. In front of you is the top of the large outside staircase to the lower floor and on the right is the entrance to the king's first-floor apartments. Go in through this door.

On the restored floor of the **Upper Hall of the Double Axes** Evans placed the bases of the door-jambs found on the floor below, where they had fallen, and he gave this hall the same arrangement as the one on the ground floor. Leave the room by a door in the south-west corner and go past the queen's Private Staircase on the left. Opposite you is the restored **Upper Hall of the Queen.** Walk across to the bench on the west wall, which is above the Dressing Room. On the right is the upper part of the Court of the Distaffs and on the left another water closet.

Now go on into the South-East Sector of the palace. In the **South-East**

40. The Grand Staircase. This landing, called the Hall of the Royal Guard, is decorated with a copy of the fresco of figure-of-eight shields. On the right is the door into the Upper Hall of the Queen.

Bathroom you can admire the clay bathtub, while in front of the entrance to the room is a low plaster barrier forming a passage where the famous Lily Jars were found (they are now on display in the Herakleion Museum). In the opposite corner there is a bench. Turn left and you come to a small room where three small storage jars were found behind a similar barrier. This entire area was filled in after the catastrophe of 1600 B.C. and another suite was built on top of it, reached by a staircase located to the east of the bathroom.

Further south is the **Shrine of the Double Axes,** a small rectangular room now roofed over. At the far end of it is a plastered bench covered with pebbles, on which were two pairs of plaster horns with a hole in the centre indicating that a double axe would have been placed between the horns. A small steatite axe, a clay figurine of the Minoan goddess with raised hands and clay figurines of votaries were also found on the bench. On the floor in front of it a three-legged plaster offering table and various vases for offerings to the goddess were found. The shrine is dated to the LM IIIB period (13th century B.C.), that is to Postpalatial times, but there is evidence that cult practices had taken place here in earlier days, too, because a libation pit and conical cups of the LM IB period were found in the deeper levels.

To the west of the Shrine of the Double Axes there is a corridor which is called the **Corridor of the Sword Tablets** on account of the clay tablets that were found in it with Linear B inscriptions referring to swords. It leads south to a wide staircase, of which a few steps have survived, and from the top of this a **Lustral Basin** can be seen on the left and a light-well on the right. Beyond the light-well and outside the actual palace are the ruins of private residences which will be described in the chapter on the dependencies of the palace. One's eye is caught by the massive stone blocks which were dislodged from the walls of the palace by the earthquake of 1600 and fell on to the neighbouring house, which is consequently called the **House of the Fallen Blocks.**

Return to the Upper Queen's Hall and go down the Service Staircase to the ground floor, coming out yet again into the Hall of the Colonnades at the bottom of the Grand Staircase.

Royal Workshops and Magazines – East Hall

From the Hall of the Colonnades go along the West-East Corridor once again, but this time continue past the entrance to the Hall of the Double Axes and on to the end of the corridor, where you go through a door on the left. Here you leave the royal Domestic Quarters and enter the north sector

41. The East Bastion, which served as the east entrance to the palace. Gutters to carry away the rain-water run alongside the stairways, with settling-tanks at intervals to allow the sediment to sink to the bottom.

of the East Wing, in which the royal workshops and magazines are to be found. The thick wall to be seen on the plan of the palace in the East Wing, on the north side of the West-East Corridor, separates the Domestic Quarters from the artisans' sector. Take the first door on the right into the **Lobby of the Wooden Posts** (a name derived from the common Minoan building system) and go through it into the **East Portico.** This is a splendid four-columned verandah overlooking the Kairatos valley. To the west of the portico is a room containing some large lumps of greenish rock: this is the renowned Spartan basalt, a rare stone brought from the Peloponnese. It would appear that we are on the ground floor of a **Lapidary's Workshop,** for two stone vases that had fallen from above were found in here. Traces of working may be discerned on the lumps of stone. Perhaps the final disaster stopped the artisan while he was actually at work on it. Further north is the room which Evans initially called the **School Room** because of the benches along the walls. More likely it was a potter's workshop: the receptacles to be seen by the benches were probably used for kneading the clay that was later used to make vases.

Leaving this room by the north door you enter the **Court of the Stone Spout,** so named after the stone spout high up on the west wall. The rain-water which was channelled through it seems eventually to have been collected in a blind well which can be seen beneath the grating outside the restored north wall of the court. Facing you, a little further north, are the **Magazines of the Giant Pithoi,** now roofed over. They comprise part of the storerooms of the Old Palace (further north still are the Royal Pottery Stores, also of Protopalatial date, in which the finest examples of Kamares ware were found). Pause to admire the huge Protopalatial storage jars, which may put you in mind of the Cretan myth of Glaukos, one of Minos' sons, who was drowned in a pithos full of honey.

Now go down the reconstructed staircase which passes in front of the Magazines of the Giant Pithoi. At the very bottom stands the **East Bastion,** marking the east entrance to the palace and at the same time the exit to the west bank of the Kairatos river, where Evans believed the bull-leaping arena was situated. The most interesting feature here is the series of open rain-water conduits which run alongside the stairways of the East Bastion. The conduits run in a parabolic curve which checks the flow of water, and at intervals there are settling-tanks in which sediment sank to the bottom and so the water was cleared. (Evans believed that this water was collected in a cistern somewhere outside the palace and was used for washing the palace laundry.)

42. *The north sector of the East Wing. In the foreground is the Court of the Stone Spout (the spout is visible near the top of the wall on the right), and behind it is the so-called "School Room", which was most probably a potter's workshop.*

43. *The north sector of the East Wing. Here we see the Room of the Stone Drainhead, in which rain-water was channelled from a clay down-pipe into the big open stone drain.*

44. General view of the
palace of Knossos from
the north-east. Clearly
visible in the foreground
is the north sector of
the East Wing, which
contained the royal
workshops and
store-rooms.

Return to the Magazines of the Giant Pithoi and go up to the top of the modern staircase, where there is a corridor (of which the south part has been restored) with a grating in the floor. This is known as the **Corridor of the Draughtboard,** for it was here that the excavators found a gaming-board used for a game rather similar to chess. The board is made of precious materials including ivory, rock crystal and faience, and ivory pawns were used with it. Beneath the grating in the floor you can see a section of the pipes which carried drinking water to the palace, most probably from a spring on Mt. Juktas a few kilometres to the south-west of Knossos. The clay pipes taper and interlock perfectly. This water supply system was dated by Evans to the time of the Old Palace. To the west of the Corridor of the Draughtboard, just beyond the foot of a staircase to the upper floor, the remnants of Evans' **North-East Hall** can be seen with two column bases still *in situ.* Further on are the **North-East Magazines.** South-east of the corridor there seems to have been a columned verandah, the **North-East Verandah** (one column base has survived with its foundations). North-east of the corridor, at a lower level, you can see a series of partitions formed of upright slabs inserted in grooves. These may perhaps have been stalls for the palace animals.

From the south end of the Corridor of the Draughtboard go into a compartment with a square stone basin, the so-called **Room of the Stone Drainhead.** Here the rain-water was collected by means of a clay down-pipe and was then channelled into a long stone conduit which can be seen running eastwards in a zig-zag under the North-East Verandah to terminate at the outlet on the west wall of the Court of the Stone Spout. West of the Room of the Stone Drainhead are two roofed areas: the **Magazine of the Medallion Pithoi** and the **Corridor of the Bays.** Go first into the long, narrow royal storeroom which took its name from the jars decorated with relief medallions. As indicated by the lower (earlier) floor with a circular stand for a large storage jar, the Magazine of the Medallion Pithoi succeeded an older one of the Protopalatial period which housed giant pithoi like those we saw a little while ago. The adjacent Corridor of the Bays is so named because it has two piers projecting from its west wall to form three deep recesses, where coarse pottery was stored. Both rooms were only used in the first phase of the New Palace (end of MM III), after which they were filled in and the door now visible leading to the Grand Staircase was blocked off. However, the thick piers which form the storage bays are not there for no reason. The Corridor of the Bays is one storey down from the level of the Central Court. Overhead, exactly in the position of the modern concrete roof, would have been the floor of Evans' **East Hall,** and the stout walls of the bays must have served to support three columns which stood in front of the Hall at the head of the broad steps leading up to it from the Central Court. The general outline of the East Hall is evident from the position of the thickest basement walls, which means that it was considerably larger than the present-day concrete cover. It occupied the entire area from the Central Court as far as the corridor west of the Lapidary's Workshop and from the Grand Staircase and its West-East Corridor as far as the

45. Reconstruction drawing of the North Entrance Passage, by Piet de Jong. The sloping passage was flanked by bastions on both sides, each with a colonnaded verandah above.

south entrance to the Corridor of the Draughtboard (or the thick wall facing the north exit of the Corridor of the Bays). It seems that the East Hall had a peristyle of eight columns around a central light-well and was decorated with magnificent relief frescoes, fragments of which (depicting griffins tethered to columns, scenes of the bull-games and other sports) were found where they had fallen on to the floor below. It is believed that it was a reception hall, and perhaps this was the actual throne room in the sense of the place where the king exercised his political authority. It is probable that a huge wooden statue of a goddess also stood in the East Hall, because a quantity of carbonised wood and three large bronze locks of hair were found outside its north wall. From here you walk up to the Central Court and cross over to the North Wing of the palace.

North Entrance – North Lustral Area – Theatral Area

From about the middle of the north side of the Central Court a long corridor leads to the North Entrance of the palace. Before starting along it, notice a complex of rooms to the west of the corridor and north of the Throne Room. In this area was the **Early Keep** or the **Dungeons,** as Evans named a group of six cells which were cut deep down into the Neolithic stratum and had no doors (most probably they were accessible through trapdoors in the floor above). The wall which surrounded these rooms was rectangular in outline, with rounded corners, which is why the complex was considered to be one of the *insulae* which, according to Evans, preceded the completed palace. The deep cells were thought to be dungeons, but they may simply have been cellars. Before the end of the Protopalatial period the dungeons were filled in and covered over with a new floor, part of which is still visible underneath the lower part of a MM II pithos. Then, in the Neopalatial period, the rooms we see today were built. Their walls were underpinned by Evans with brick arches so that the dungeons should remain visible. The Neopalatial complex includes a shrine with a gypsum floor and a square pillar base in the centre (most probably a sacred Pillar Crypt), the Room of the Saffron Gatherer Fresco and the Room of the Stirrup Jars, where clay Linear B tablets were discovered together with LM IIIB stirrup jars, giving rise to the controversy over the dating of the Linear B tablets at Knossos. From the area above the shrine came the miniature frescoes of the Sacred Grove and the Tripartite Shrine, copies of which we have seen in the restored room with the light-well, above the Throne Room.

We now enter the **North Entrance Passage,** which is a steep open-air ramp with a paved floor. It was originally wider, but in the Neopalatial period its width was reduced by the construction of bastions on both sides, each with a colonnaded verandah above. A staircase on the left leads up to the verandah of the **West Bastion,** which has been restored and adorned with a replica of the relief fresco of the Bull in an Olive Grove (the subject was probably the capture of a bull). On the walls of the bastion below the verandah the trident symbol is incised with remarkable frequency (perhaps because this passage led to the seaward exit of the palace). If we accept Evans' view that the fresco of the bull was preserved *in situ* on top of the ruins for many years after the destruction of the palace, we can imagine the effect it would have had in formulating the myth of the Minotaur and the Labyrinth.

At the north end of the ramp, on the east side, there is a narrow room with a door (the gypsum bases of the door-jambs have survived), from

46. The restored West Bastion of the North Entrance Passage, with a copy of the relief fresco of the Bull in an Olive Grove.

which there may have been a wooden staircase to the upper storey. Facing you at the bottom of the ramp is a large oblong room containing two rows of four square piers and one round column. This is the **North Pillar Hall,** and on its west side is the double outer gate which was the North Entrance to the palace. Evans named the Pillar Hall the "Customs House" because he believed that it was here that merchandise was inspected on its arrival from the harbour. Careful study of the area and comparison with the Kitchen at Zakros has led Professor J.W. Graham to suggest that the Banquet Hall probably stood immediately above the Pillar Hall. This view is supported by the existence of several storage rooms in the North-East Sector, and more especially by the fact that various domestic utensils, sorted according to type, were found in the neighbouring North-East Magazines. A hypothetical reconstruction of the Banquet Hall gives it a rectangular floor plan with two rows of five columns placed directly on top of the piers and columns of the ground floor. The guests would have reached the hall by way of the two bastion verandahs. The wooden staircase whose existence was surmised off to the east from the end of the North Entrance Passage would have been the service staircase leading up directly from the Kitchen, and there was presumably another stairway

coming from the servants' quarters to the east.

Outside the palace, about 20 metres north of the Pillar Hall, is the **North Pillar Crypt,** perhaps a cult place. Still visible in it are two monolithic square pillars and the bases of another two, which obviously supported a large hall in the upper storey.

Leave the palace by the North Gate and go towards the restored **North Lustral Area,** recognisable by its protective roof. The lustral basin here is large and deeper than the other ones we have seen so far. It has steps on three sides, columns on a parapet on two sides and similar columns on the balustrade of the staircase leading down to it. It is built of ashlared limestone blocks with a dado of gypsum slabs on the walls and gypsum floor paving. Above the dado the walls were painted with a design imitating sponge impressions. Inside the basin the excavators found a beautiful stone ewer and a number of small clay jugs which were believed to have contained myrrh for use in the ritual purification and anointing. Around the basin there is a large enclosure which Evans called the **Initiatory Area,** where the lid of a stone bowl bearing the cartouche of Khyan, one of the Hyksos kings of Egypt, was found; this made it possible for the associated MM IIIA pottery to be dated to the end of the 17th century B.C. A double door leads from the Lustral Area into a room which, in turn, communicates through a triple door with the **North-West Portico** (which has a double door of its own in the north wall). From the North-West Portico there is a way into the palace along a dog-leg ramp with steps at intervals, leading to the Corridor of the Stone Basin and from there either to the Central Court or to the West Magazines. Evans believed that the Lustral Basin and the Initiatory Area were designed to prepare and purify all those who went along this route to the West Magazines of the Sanctuary.

Now proceed to the **Theatral Area,** which lies outside the palace not far from the north-west corner. It consists of a paved court which is traversed by a raised Processional Way and is bordered by steps on its east and south sides. At the south-east corner of the Theatre, in the angle between the two banks of steps, there is a bastion-like structure which is believed to have been a sort of royal box for the king and his family. We can imagine the monarch sitting there, surrounded by as many as 500 members of his court standing on the low steps, and watching the games, dances or religious rites or receiving official guests, or even, perhaps,

◄ *47. The North Entrance Passage leads to the North Pillar Hall, which Evans called the "Customs House" because he believed that it was used for the inspection of merchandise arriving from the harbour.*

48. The North Lustral Area, containing the largest and deepest of all the lustral basins in the palace of Knossos.

49. The Theatral Area, a paved court traversed by a raised Processional Way and bounded on two sides by broad banks of steps with the "royal box" in the angle between them. The restored North Lustral Area is visible in the background.

meting out justice. If you go up to the top of the steps on the east side you can see behind the Theatral Area what remains of the preceding architectural phases: originally a paved court existed here with a *kouloura* like those in the West Court (the pit was found beneath the north wall of the Theatral Area but is no longer visible). At a later date the new floor was laid, with raised Processional Ways, and then the tiers of steps were built. The Processional Way which crosses the paving of the Theatral Area continues westwards through part of the town (a number of houses, including the "Arsenal" and the House of the Frescoes, have been found on both sides of the road) and ran as far as the environs of the Little Palace. It was called the **Royal Road** and it is possible to imagine that on feast-days a procession would have set off from the Little Palace, following the route which has been described as "the oldest road in Europe", to the Theatral Area. Another raised walk passes behind the southern steps of the Theatral Area and on past the large Horns of Consecration to the North Entrance, while a diagonal offshoot to the north-east perhaps led to the North Pillar Crypt. Yet another branch to the south, most probably stepped at the beginning, led to the West Court of the palace: it skirted the entire length of the West Facade, passed in front of the stone altars and terminated at the **West Porch,** the ceremonial entrance to the palace.

So we find ourselves back where we began our visit to the palace of Minos. We have seen many of the rooms and tried to envisage it as it was when it was alive. It may be that we have understood much less than we had hoped, and perhaps we have imagined many things quite differently from the way they actually were 3,500 years ago. We may be tired and confused, but nevertheless we are sure to be filled with boundless wonder at this Labyrinth of 1,500 rooms, for no matter how many times we visit it we shall always discover something extra and find some new question to set us thinking. Scholars of the future will add much and alter much of what is now accepted. However, nothing can alter our admiration for the way of life in those distant days, as illustrated in the wall-paintings and as indicated by the rooms in the palace. The palace of Knossos was full of movement, and life there was varied, polished and closely bound up with nature and simple pleasures.

THE DEPENDENCIES OF THE PALACE

The palace was surrounded by a whole city which still awaits excavation. The only ruins laid bare up to now have been royal villas and buildings believed to have been the residences of officials directly connected with the palace. (Some of them are shown on the Plan of the Environs of the Palace and others on the Plan of the Palace of Knossos).

The **House of the Frescoes** is located to the south of the Royal Road,

50. The Theatral Area from the south. On the ground in front of the southern bank of steps is a large fragment of a pair of "horns of consecration".

behind the ruins of the ground floor of another house. It is a simple little house with a lovely floor in the south-east corner room (plaster border round an ironstone centre). The house is interesting on account of its fine wall-paintings, which were not found lying in disorder, having fallen from the walls, but had been neatly and deliberately stacked in one part of the oblong central room. Fragile layers of painted plaster, barely 4 mm. thick, were found piled one on top of the other. They depict royal gardens and the Blue Bird, the Blue Monkey and the Captain of the Blacks.

Outside the South-East Sector of the palace there are (reading from south-west to north-east) the House of the Sacrificed Oxen, the House of the Fallen Blocks, the House of the Chancel Screen, the South-East House and the Monolithic Pillar Basement.

The **House of the Sacrificed Oxen** and the **House of the Fallen Blocks** were both built at the same time as the New Palace in MM III and were destroyed by the great earthquake at the end of that period (1600 B.C.). Only the basements remain. In the westernmost house were found the skulls of two bulls which had obviously been sacrificed, together with portable altars, which may be interpreted as evidence of a sacred rite to appease the divinity who caused the earthquakes. In the adjacent house one can see the huge blocks that fell from the South Front of the palace and demolished it.

Immediately to the east, almost touching the corner of the palace, stands the **House of the Chancel Screen,** which has been partially roofed. Only the ground floor has survived. There are three storerooms, a Pillar Crypt and a Lustral Basin. The entrance was somewhere on the east side with a staircase leading up from it to the central hall, which has another hall opening off it to the north. This latter hall has a paved floor and on its west side there is a balustrade with a central gateway flanked by two columns. Behind the balustrade two steps lead to a raised dais on which stands a base for a throne or an altar. This arrangement led the workmen engaged on the excavation to name it the "Priest's House", and we shall see a similar chancel-like structure in two other buildings outside the palace, the House of the High Priest and the Royal Villa.

The **South-East House** lies below the House of the Chancel Screen. To reach it you go down two flights of stairs, which bring you out into a corridor. On your left is a crypt with a single pillar and a sunken cist in the floor. Here were found two stands for double axes and a beautiful tall porphyry lamp; a niche in the west wall was perhaps for offerings. In the centre of the house there is a rectangular room with three of its walls built of ashlar limestone blocks (a type of masonry rarely used for internal walls) with a gypsum facing, while on the fourth side there is a partition wall of gypsum slabs. Opening off it to the south is a small paved court with a

51, 52. The House of the Chancel Screen. Beyond the balustrade, with its central gateway flanked by two columns, two steps lead up to a dais for a throne or an altar.

peristyle of three columns and a triple door on the west leading to another room with a gypsum dado on its walls.

North of this house, near the east side of the palace, there is a kiln which was probably used for smelting ore. Above it is the east facade of the palace and nearby is the **Monolithic Pillar Basement,** all that remains of another Minoan house. It contains two tall, monolithic, square pillars and has four bays on the opposite wall. Presumably the walls of the bays supported the upper storey.

Near the south-west corner of the palace stands the **South House.** We know that it was built after the catastrophe of 1600 B.C. because its west wall stands on the ruins of the Stepped Portico, which prior to the earthquake led up to the South-West Entrance to the palace. Parts of the ground floor and two upper storeys have survived and there may have been a third floor. It has been partially restored. The entrance was most probably situated in the south-east corner, but nowadays you go directly from the remains of the Stepped Portico into the second floor, where the column is, and from there you come down to the first floor. You are now in a pillar crypt in which there is a stand for a double axe and another for sacred objects (perhaps horns). From here you should go towards the north-east corner of the house, where you will find the Main Hall with a lovely paved floor, an antechamber to the south (leading to the probable entrance area) and a bathroom to the west. A staircase starting from the corridor to the south of the bathroom takes you down to the ground floor. Note the door-jambs here, which are monolithic pieces of gypsum. You can still see evidence of the mechanism for bolting the door, which consisted of a wooden bar that slotted into a socket in the jamb and was secured by a bronze pin. Two rooms were found on the ground floor, one with three square pillars in a row and the other containing bronze tools and double axes. Back on the first floor, note the staircase which continued up to the second floor, the room with a row of column bases on top of the ground-floor pillars and, next to that, another room off which there is a smaller chamber that may have been a washroom, with a latrine in the corner.

These are the most important buildings in the immediate environs of the palace. There still remains the **North-West House,** which was discovered in the West Court between the *kouloures* and the Theatral Area and was dubbed the North-West Treasure House on account of the bronzes found there. It was filled in after being excavated and is not visible today. Then there is the **North-East House,** of which several storerooms were found near the north-east corner of the palace. There are also remains of various buildings (some later than the palace) to the south of the West Court.

We conclude with a description of the buildings outside the archaeological site of the palace, which cannot be visited without a special permit. From the East Bastion of the palace a three-minute walk to the north brings you to the **Royal Villa.** It is built in a cutting in the hillside and faces eastwards over the valley of the river Kairatos. The ground floor has survived and part of the first floor has been restored, and there was origi-

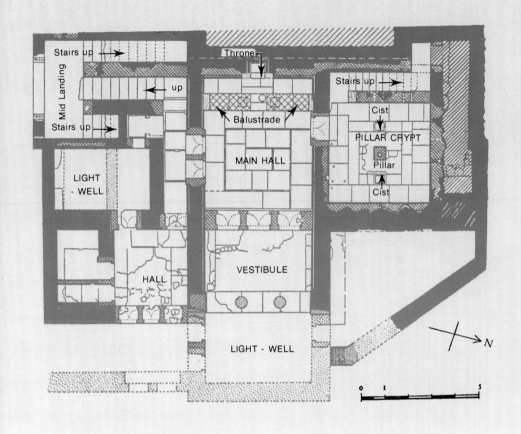

53. The Royal Villa (after Sir A. Evans).

nally a second floor as well. Entering by way of a light-well, you go through a vestibule into the Main Hall. The walls are faced with gypsum slabs and the floor is paved with the same material. On the west side of the room there is an imposing balustrade with a central doorway flanked by two columns. Three steps lead to a raised dais on which, in a recess in the centre of the opposite wall, there probably stood a kind of throne which was lit from above by a light-well. Opening off the main hall to the north is a crypt with a square pillar in the centre. This is the best preserved of all the Pillar Crypts, with walls of ashlared gypsum blocks and a gypsum-paved floor in which there are channels around the pillar and two sunken cists to catch the blood or libations offered to the deity. Note the sockets high on the wall to hold the rafters of the ceiling, which were originally whole tree-trunks (concrete copies of the rafters have now been installed). A staircase led from the crypt to the upper floor from which, without being seen, one could communicate orally via the light-well with the person

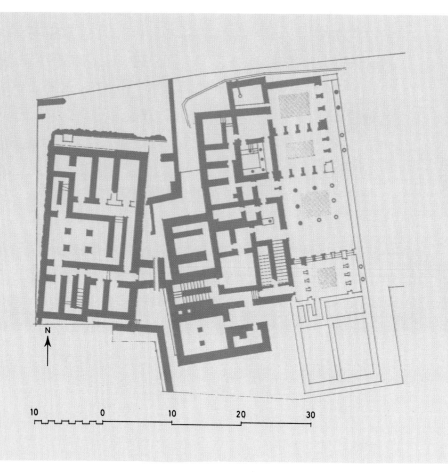

54. The Little Palace and the Unexplored Mansion (after M. Popham).

sitting on the throne behind the chancel screen. It would appear that the overall layout had some special significance and the house is altogether unusual: there are no storerooms on the ground floor; it is not a large house yet the construction is luxurious, copious use being made of gypsum; it is in direct communication with the palace; and it stands in a privileged position in the valley of the river. It seems that it was intended to be used by the king for some special purpose. A double door in the south wall of the main hall opens into a corridor giving access in one direction to the south-east corner of the house, which may have been the living quarters (note the partition wall of double upright slabs of gypsum) and in the other direction, through a door under the stairs, to a light-well which obviously illuminated the upper storeys. Alternatively you could go past the door under the stairs and up the staircase to the first floor. This stairway is unique: it starts with a single flight, which branches at the halfway landing into two parallel flights both leading to the first-floor landing, from which a fourth flight, directly above the first, leads to the second floor.

The **Little Palace** is located to the west of the modern road from Knossos to Herakleion, a very short distance away from the main palace. The entrance was on the east side and led into a vestibule, from which a pier-and-door partition with three broad steps led up into a peristyle court to the north. In the north part of the court was another multiple door leading into the Main Hall, itself divided into two rooms by a pier-and-door partition and opening on to a columned verandah to the east. Note the fine paved floor of the Main Hall (crazy paving surrounded by gypsum flagstones, similar to some of the floors in the palace of Knossos) and the gypsum dado on the walls. Behind the north part of the Hall is a washroom with an outlet to the drain outside the building, while behind the south section is the roofed Lustral Basin, which after the destruction of Knossos, in the so-called "Reoccupation Period" (LM IIIB), was used as a Fetish Shrine, as indicated by the natural stalagmitic formations found there. At that time the spaces between the columns of the balustrade were walled up and the impressions of the columns preserved on the mud-brick infill show us that they were fluted, with fifteen grooves. In the centre of the Little Palace there is a large roofed staircase of two flights which led to the upper floor. At the south end of the building were the Pillar Crypts: one in the south-west corner and two others in the basement at the south-east corner.

Just behind the Little Palace is the building of which Evans revealed only the east facade, which he called the **Unexplored Mansion.** It has now been excavated. It was connected with the Little Palace by a bridge and had a very fine ashlar facade and staircases to the upper storey. The most important room is the central hall with its ashlar masonry and four pillars. The Mansion was built in the LM IA period but was also inhabited in LM II - LM IIIA1, as is indicated by added walls in the central hall which date from the time of the Mycenaean dynasty at Knossos. It was destroyed by fire ca. 1375 B.C., but there is evidence indicating that it was re-used in later times.

Following the Herakleion-Knossos road southwards, go on past the large palace until you come to a signpost on the left pointing to the **Caravanserai**, as Evans characteristically named the guest-house. Two rooms facing the palace have been restored. The eastern room is like a porch and its interior walls were decorated with the famous Partridge Fresco, a copy of which has been placed in its original position. The style of the painting is reminiscent of those in the House of the Frescoes. In the next room there was a stone water-tank which, according to Evans, was where the travellers washed their feet.

Near the Caravanserai is the **Spring Chamber,** which has been roofed and restored. Three gypsum steps lead to a rectangular room with a gypsum dado. Facing the entrance are two high ledges with a niche for an oil lamp between them. In the floor there was a small pool with well-worn steps leading down to it. The Chamber was found full of pottery, ashes and offerings dating from Minoan and Sub-Minoan times, which indicates that the spring was used as a shrine.

55. *The Little Palace of Knossos. The restored room contains a large staircase of two flights leading to the upper floor.*

56. *The Unexplored Mansion is situated next to the Little Palace, with a bridge linking the two buildings.*

57. *The Royal Villa. The staircase up from the ground floor starts with a single flight to the halfway landing; there it branches into two flights, both leading up in the reverse direction to the first-floor landing, from which a fourth flight, directly above the first, led to the second floor.*

57

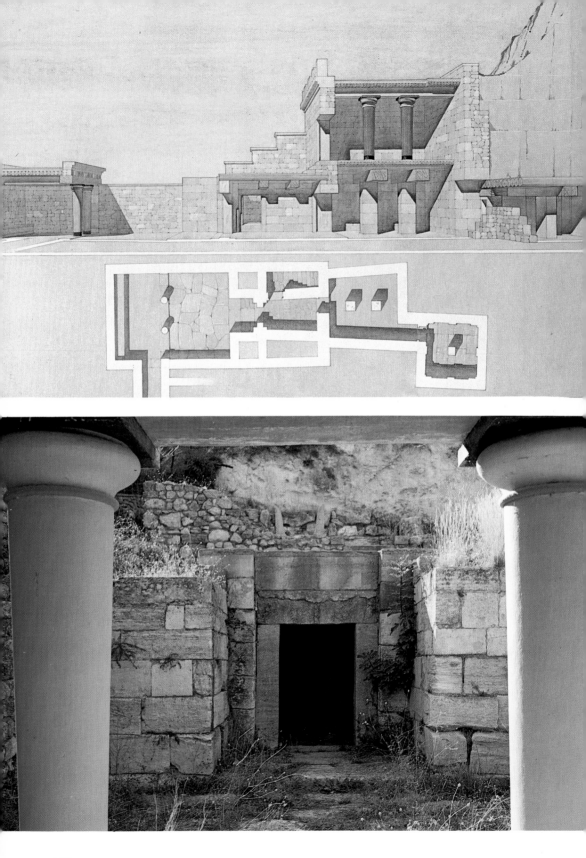

If you go a little way down the hillside along a narrow path, you come to the four massive piers of the Minoan **Viaduct** over the Vlychia stream, a tributary of the Kairatos. They are built of huge blocks of stone and the tallest still stands to a height of eight courses. Between the piers there are four or five steps going down to the water level. This viaduct carried the road leading from Southern Crete to Knossos. The traveller coming from the south would rest awhile at the Caravanserai, cross the bridge and then walk up the Stepped Portico to the South-West Entrance to the palace.

The **House of the High Priest** is situated to the south of the Caravanserai, on your left as you walk southwards and below the road. There is very little left of the house, which owes its name to the altar which was found there. In the ruins you can see a balustrade with a central gateway flanked by two columns. Behind this there are two chests to right and left of the gateway, and four steps lead to the raised dais on which, in a deep square recess, a biconcave stone altar was found, flanked by stands for double axes. In front of the altar there is a hole leading down to a stone drain, probably for pouring libations.

A little further south and to the west of the main road stands the **Temple Tomb**. It was partially restored by Evans but in any case its ashlar masonry is very well preserved. The structure presents an interesting combination of tomb and temple. The entrance is on the north side of the two-columned portico which leads into a paved court. Opposite the portico is a gateway between two bastions, leading into an inner hall. Inside the inner hall, on the left, is the entrance to the staircase which led to the temple at the upper level, and facing you is the entrance to the Pillar Crypt, which could be locked by the same method as was employed in the South House. Inside the crypt Evans found an ossuary which he thought had been made to receive the bones of persons killed in the earthquake of 1600 B.C. In the north-west corner of the crypt is the entrance to the tomb-chamber, which is hewn out of the soft rock, with a square central pillar and gypsum slabs facing the walls. The roof — which was the natural rock — was painted blue, the colour of the sky. The body was probably interred in a wooden *larnax* (coffin), which has perished. Nevertheless, a subsequent burial of the LM II period has survived, for the bodies of a short middle-aged man and a child were found interred in a small pit in the north-east corner of the chamber. Was this perhaps the last king of Knossos? It may not be too fanciful to think so. The staircase from the inner hall leads up to a terrace above it, which gives access to the temple with its two columns on top of the square piers of the Pillar Crypt. The layout of the tomb brings to mind Diodorus Siculus' description of Minos' tomb in Sicily, which was said to have a temple of Aphrodite above the actual tomb-chamber.

58. The Temple Tomb. Ground plan and reconstruction by Piet de Jong.

59. The Temple Tomb. Between the two bastions is the entrance to the inner hall.

60, 61. *The Royal Villa. Two views of the main hall: one (60) looking towards the vestibule and light-well, the other (61) showing the colonnaded balustrade and the door into the pillar crypt.*

62. *The Royal Villa. The pillar crypt, with its central square pillar surrounded by channels in the floor and with two sunken cists which were probably put there to catch the blood of sacrificial victims or libations offered to the deity.*

62

ART TREASURES FROM KNOSSOS

63. The priceless bull's head rhyton from the Little Palace of Knossos. This magnificent libation vessel was carved from a block of black steatite, with horns of gilded wood, eyes of inlaid rock crystal and jasper and nostrils of mother-of-pearl. Ca. 1550-1500 B.C. Herakleion Museum.

64. Faience plaque depicting a wild goat suckling her young, from the Temple Repositories in the palace of Knossos. Ca. 1600 B.C. Herakleion Museum.

65, 66. The famous faience statuettes of the snake goddesses, from the Temple Repositories in the palace of Knossos. Ca. 1600 B.C. Herakleion Museum.

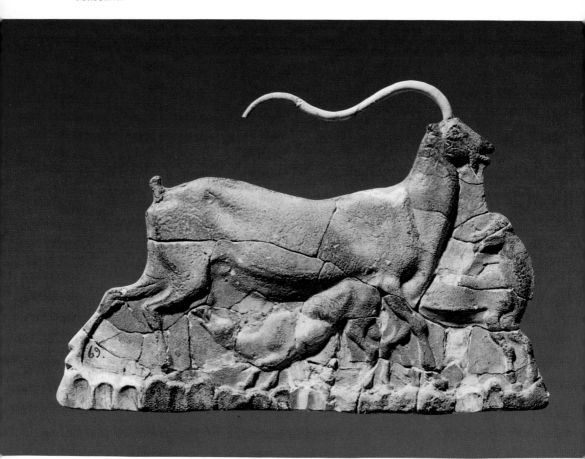

67. *Detail from the Fresco of the Procession, which gave its name to the corridor leading from the West Court to the South Propylaeum. Young Minoans carrying ritual vessels. 15th cent. B.C. Herakleion Museum.*

68. *Another branch of the Corridor of the Procession led to the Central Court, and the relief fresco of the Prince of the Lilies most probably adorned the final stretch of this section of the corridor. It depicts a regal figure, probably the Priest-King, wearing a crown of lilies and peacock plumes. With his outstretched left hand he may have been leading a sphinx or a griffin. Ca. 1550 B.C. Herakleion Museum.*

67

69. *The celebrated Minoan lady known as "La Parisienne", part of the Camp Stool Fresco, which was probably painted on the wall of the Sanctuary Hall on the Piano Nobile. The sacral knot worn at the back of the neck seems to indicate that she is a priestess or even a goddess. Ca. 1400 B.C. Herakleion Museum.*

70. *The Bull-Leaping Fresco, which comes from the East Wing of the palace, shows the three successive stages of the sport and thus gives us a full and clear picture of how it was performed. As the bull charges, the acrobat first grasps its horns, then somersaults on to its back and finally jumps off. Both men and women took part in this hazardous sport. 15th cent. B.C. Herakleion Museum.*

70

71

72

71. *Detail from the Dolphin Fresco, which was painted on the wall of the Queen's Hall in the palace of Knossos. Ca. 1600 B.C. Herakleion Museum.*

72. *Detail from the Partridge Frieze found in the Caravanserai, a small building south of the palace. Ca. 1500 B.C. Herakleion Museum.*

73. *The Blue Bird Fresco from the House of the Frescoes, north-west of the palace of Knossos. The bird is shown in a setting of veined rocks, surrounded by irises and wild roses. Ca. 1550 B.C. Herakleion Museum.*

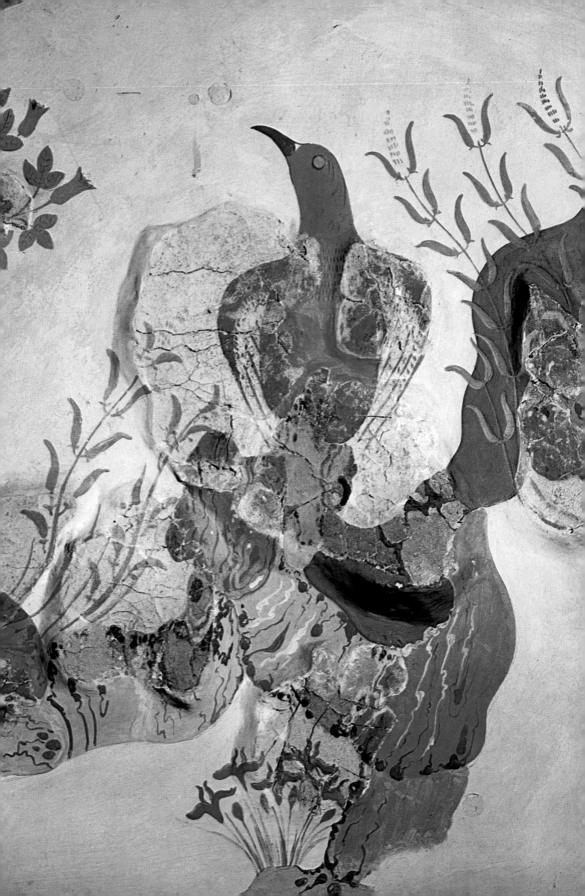

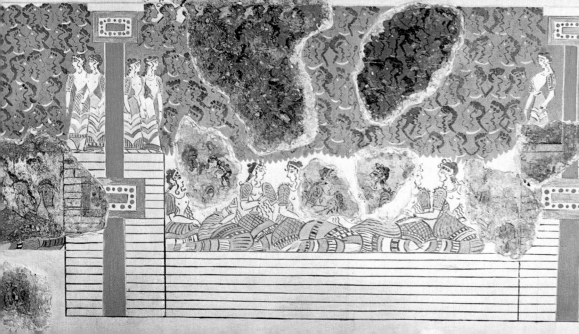

74, 75. *After 1600* B.C.
*a trend set in at
Knossos for the painting
of miniature frescoes,
with human figures and
buildings all depicted
on a very small scale.
The subjects are often
connected with religious
rites, as is the case
with these two parts of
the miniature fresco of
the Tripartite Shrine.
Herakleion Museum.*

76. *The Cup-Bearer,
part of the fresco
depicting a religious
procession, adorned the
walls of the South
Propylaeum. 15th cent.*
B.C. *Herakleion
Museum.*

77. *Sealstones of the Neopalatial period from the palace of Knossos. A pair of bulls, a lioness attacking a bull and a goddess standing between two griffins are typical examples of the subjects that were minutely carved on hard gemstones. Herakleion Museum.*

78. *A gold ring from the tomb of Isopata, near Knossos, showing a religious scene which may represent an ecstatic ritual dance and an "epiphany" of a goddess. Ca. 1500 B.C. Herakleion Museum.*

79. *Gold earrings from the necropolis of Mavro Spilio, near Knossos. Shortly after 1400 B.C. Herakleion Museum.*

80. *A priceless pendant of gold and rock crystal from the tholos tomb at Chaniali Tekke, near Knossos. 7th cent. B.C. Herakleion Museum.*

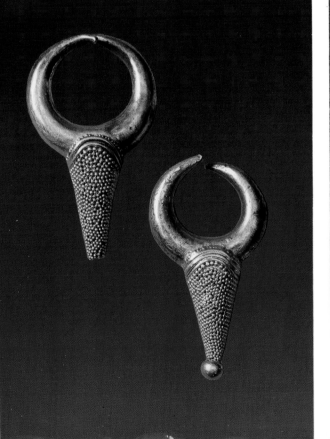

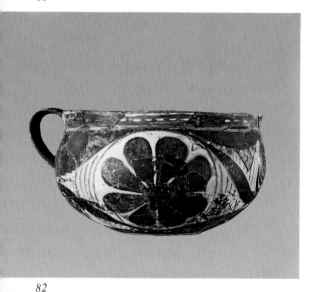

81, 82. Two finds from Knossos dating from the period of the old palace: a cup of eggshell Kamares ware (81) and an amphora decorated with palm trees in the late Kamares style (82). Herakleion Museum.

83. A three-handled amphora in the so-called "Palace Style" from a tomb at Katsambas (the port area of Knossos), decorated with boar's-tusk helmets. 1425-1400 B.C. Herakleion Museum.

84. Libation jug with beaked spout, a particularly accomplished piece of work with painted and relief decoration, from one of the Katsambas tombs. Late Neopalatial period, ca. 1400 B.C. Herakleion Museum.

82

83

85. *This statuette of a goddess with upraised arms comes from the Shrine of the Double Axes in the palace of Knossos. Postpalatial period, 13th cent.* B.C. *Herakleion Museum.*